LAST WITNESSES
in the
BUNKER

LAST WITNESSES
in the
BUNKER

Pierre Galante & Eugène Silianoff

Translated from the French by Jan Dalley

SIDGWICK & JACKSON
LONDON

Contents

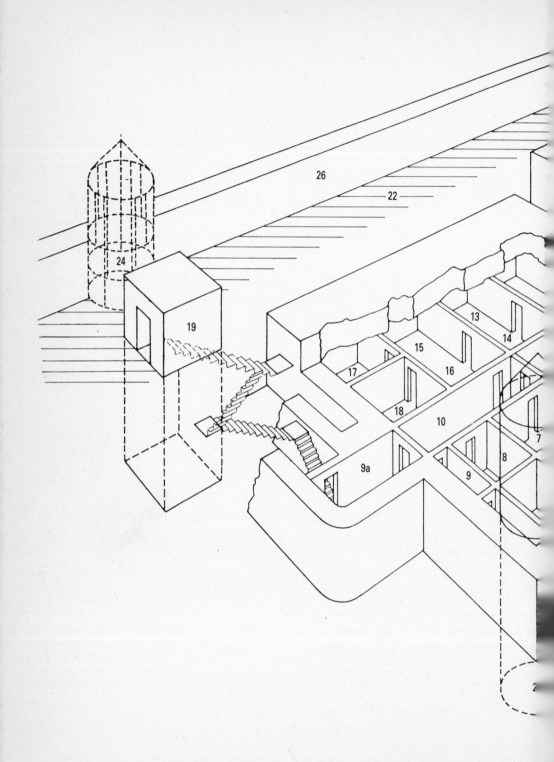

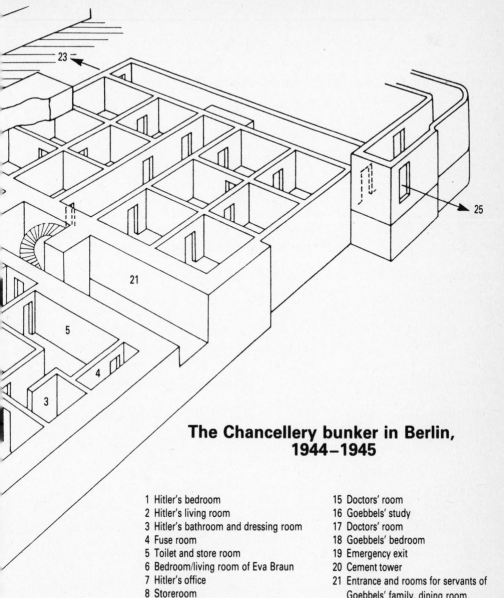

The Chancellery bunker in Berlin, 1944–1945

1 Hitler's bedroom
2 Hitler's living room
3 Hitler's bathroom and dressing room
4 Fuse room
5 Toilet and store room
6 Bedroom/living room of Eva Braun
7 Hitler's office
8 Storeroom
9 Guardroom and dressing room
9a Hitler's personal guard's room
10 Anterooms
11 Anterooms
12 Generator, air-filtering machines
13 Telephone switchboard
14 Telephone switchboard, Bormann's study

15 Doctors' room
16 Goebbels' study
17 Doctors' room
18 Goebbels' bedroom
19 Emergency exit
20 Cement tower
21 Entrance and rooms for servants of Goebbels' family, dining room, kitchen, Hitler's dietetic kitchen
22 Surface of the Chancellery garden
23 Towards the Foreign Ministry garden
24 Unfinished cement tower
25 Towards the new Chancellery
26 Garden wall

Foreword

In 1981 when Pierre Galante wrote *Operation Valkyrie* in collaboration with Eugène Silianoff and General Adolf Heusinger (who was present at the conference on 20 July 1944 when the attempt to assassinate Hitler took place), he was advised by the General to speak to Traudl Junge, one of Hitler's secretaries, as she had also been there at that time and could give her version of the events.

Eugène Silianoff went to Munich to interview Frau Junge and during this visit she showed to him an unpublished manuscript relating her memories and impressions, from the time she became the Führer's secretary in January 1943 until the last days in the bunker and her escape after the suicide of Hitler and Eva Braun. He read the manuscript and found it fascinating but Mrs Junge refused to agree to its publication. It was only after much thought, hesitation and discussion that she changed her mind, entrusted the document to him and finally also agreed to put him in touch with Major Otto Günsche, one of the Führer's aides-de-camp (who had been the best man at her marriage to Hans Junge). Eugène Silianoff was subsequently able to interview Hans Baur, once Hitler's private pilot, now in his nineties, who was present in the bunker for the last two days.

In several further interviews, Traudl Junge completed her story with the description of her travels across occupied Germany, her arrest by the Russians, her return to Munich and arrest by the Americans and, after her release, the difficult first steps towards forming a new life.

Frau Junge's testimonial describes exactly what life in the bunker was like, day by day, until the apocalyptic end. The reader will see in the figure of Hitler an altogether different man from

ix

the accepted image – a Jekyll-and-Hyde character who was both diabolical and pitiless in conducting the war but charming and indulgent towards his intimate circle.

The accounts given by Günsche, Baur and above all by Frau Junge illuminate a new aspect of that dark and tragic era and we feel it necessary to publish them for the sake of future generations.

Introduction

In the eyes of most foreign observers and in the opinion of anyone with access to objective information, the year 1943 was the beginning of the end of the Third Reich, but the average German was still living under the illusions of the first two euphoric years, when the Wehrmacht had marched in triumph across the European continent. On 22 June 1941, when Hitler launched Barbarossa, his attack against Russia – planned since 1940, not long after his September 1939 pact of friendship with Moscow – the map of Europe showed a striking reflection of the might of the Third Reich. Almost the entire continent, from the Atlantic to the Balkans, was occupied by German troops. Of the rest, Albania became an Italian protectorate, and three other countries - Romania, Hungary and Bulgaria – had joined the Axis alliance. Portugal and Franco's Spain, though nominally neutral, were favourable to the Axis. Apart from Switzerland there were only two truly neutral countries in Europe, at the northern and southern extremities – Sweden and Turkey – but neither had any illusions about their chances of opposing the Germans, however timidly.

Hitler reigned as absolute master over this immense expanse of territory, and when the radio announced the entry of his troops into the Soviet Union few Germans had a moment's doubt about their victory. The Führer had assembled the most powerful army in modern history on the borders of Russia: 146 divisions containing more than 3 million fighting men, 600,000 motor vehicles and 2000 planes (3000 according to Soviet sources) ready to support the land troops.

How Stalin could have been ignorant of the intentions of this colossal concentration of troops, those armaments trundling across half of Europe and the armada of planes which blotted out the sky before massing on the very frontiers of his empire, remains one of the enigmas of that war – particularly since he did not lack precise information. This was supplied partly by Churchill – but Stalin saw in Churchill only the capitalist enemy who wanted to sow discord between himself and Hitler – and partly by Richard Sorge, the German Communist spy secretly working for the USSR while attached to the German embassy in Tokyo. He was eventually executed by the Japanese, and is celebrated as a hero in the Soviet Union today.

On 20 and 21 June, immediately before the attack on the USSR, General Guderian, commander of one of the German armies, made a last inspection of his section of the front. He was amazed by the atmosphere of calm. As he wrote in *Memories of a Soldier*: 'We could see into the courtyard of the fortress of Brest-Litovsk, where the Russian soldiers were exercising by marching to music. The fortifications all along the banks of the Bug were deserted, and the work on them had made little progress during the last few weeks. . . .' Another extraordinary fact is often quoted: at 2 a.m. on the night of 21–22 June – the attack took place at 4.15 a.m. – the last train laden with Russian grain destined for Germany under the terms of the agreement between the two dictatorships passed over the railway bridge at Brest-Litovsk, its lights blazing.

Guderian knew the region well. He had been there on an official visit with an armoured brigade on 22 September 1939, when the two countries, about to become official allies, were sharing out the spoils of Poland and establishing a demarcation line. There was a common parade and an exchange of flags: the hammer and sickle on one side and the swastika on the other. Successive toasts in vodka led up to an extraordinary Freudian slip on the part of the Soviet General Krivoshin: stammering through his speech in laborious German, he said, '*Ich trinke auf die ewige Feindschaft* [instead of *Freundschaft*]. . . .' – 'I drink to the eternal enmity [instead of friendship] of our two peoples. . . .'

The opening of the campaign saw an unprecedented series of victories. The trio of field marshals – von Leeb, von Bock and von Rundstedt – who had achieved victory over France commanded three groups of forces (North, Centre and South) which penetrated the immense spaces of Russia with the same baffling ease. Three weeks after the initial attack, the German Army of the Centre was 300 miles from Moscow. By 1 July

300,000 prisoners and more than 3000 tanks had already been taken, and the battle of the Ukraine ended on 25 September with the obliteration of Marshal Budenny's armies and the capture of 655,000 prisoners, 200 tanks and more than 3700 guns. The *Blitz- krieg* of Poland and France seemed to be repeating itself: on the day of the attack Hitler had confided to the Prince of Württemberg, 'I'll be in Moscow in two or three weeks, then I'll take the Ukraine and the Caucasus. . . .'

Nazi propaganda attributed these victories entirely to Hitler, who was then proclaimed as 'the greatest strategist in history'. These superlatives about the Führer's genius in every field were repeated so often that they used to be ironically shortened in conversation to '*Gröfaz*' – *Grösster Feldherr aller Zeiten* (the Greatest Man of All Time). Such eulogies did not necessarily mean any more than the panegyrics habitually addressed to dictators, but the early campaigns of the war had left even the warlords of the traditional Prussian school speechless. In private they had dismissed Hitler's battle plans as the crazy improvisations of an amateur who knew nothing about the art of warfare, but they had seen his strategies miraculously crowned with success.

In the course of the next few years, however, his luck changed, and the criticisms were revived with renewed vigour at each new defeat. On the eve of the débâcle, in 1945, Goering himself declared, after having been dismissed by the Führer, that the archives of the war should be destroyed, so future generations would not learn that it had been directed by a madman. But in 1941 and 1942 those who had criticised Hitler's plans on the grounds that they contravened the laws of classic strategy had been forced to eat their words. Hitler had accused them of being narrow-minded, blinkered by their out-of-date views and incapable of adapting themselves to the revolutionary changes of a brilliant strategist, and the facts seemed to prove him right. Those who persevered in their belief that an evil genius was leading Germany to her downfall were less and less numerous; besides, such people were speedily eliminated. General Halder, Chief of the General Staff, was relieved of his command in the autumn of 1942 because as an experienced professional soldier he recommended breaking off the Russian campaign; soon afterwards neither Field Marshal von Leeb, Field Marshal von Bock nor the commander-in-chief, Field Marshal von Brauchitsch, was still in his former position.

In spite of the overall halt of the German offensive, 1942 saw some successes. In North Africa Rommel took Tobruk on 20 June, captured 25,000 British prisoners and pushed through Egypt as far as the gates of Alexandria. In the east von Manstein conquered the Crimea and took Sebastopol, and with renewed optimism Hitler prepared for a second offensive on Moscow. But the wheel turned definitively in 1943.

Few people today know that under the monarchy Stalingrad was called Tsaritsin (the town of the Tsarina). Renamed in honour of Stalin, it had become a symbolic stake in the game, defended – and attacked – with an ardour hardly justified by its strategic importance. Hitler's relentless refusal to allow General Paulus to try to extricate his encircled and besieged 6th Army is well known. He went so far as to promote him to the rank of field marshal on the eve of his capitulation, and many people have attributed an ulterior motive to him in doing so: since it was unprecedented for a Prussian field marshal to sign a surrender, Hitler may have been relying on this last-minute promotion to encourage Paulus to fight to the death, or perhaps to commit suicide rather than give himself up. But the result was exactly the opposite: the Russians were able to put a field marshal at the top of the list of twenty-two generals whom they had taken prisoner.

The day after his promotion, on 31 January 1943, Paulus surrendered without resistance and in a state of utter collapse; various other sections of his army surrendered cver the next few days. It is difficult to put exact numbers on the German losses because of the problem of establishing how many were killed, how many died from cold and hunger, and how many were taken prisoner but never returned. In his book *Lost Victories*, Field Marshal von Manstein conscientiously supplies a list of divisions who 'disappeared', followed by their numbers: there are twenty of them. According to Russian estimates, 140,000 Germans died at Stalingrad from various causes, not counting those taken prisoner.

A series of catastrophes on every front followed the rout at Stalingrad. The latter is usually regarded as the great turning-point of the war because of its symbolic value, and one forgets that elsewhere Hitler had been on the defensive since the previous autumn: El Alamein was fought in October 1942, and the British counter-offensive in North Africa began in November. In May 1943 Rommel's armies capitulated, and the number of prisoners - 252,000 Germans and Italians – was similar to those taken at Stalingrad, although their imprisonment would have seemed a blessing compared to the fate of those who went to Soviet camps.

After Africa, Hitler lost Italy; July brought the downfall of Mussolini and the dissolution of the Fascist party. The events in Italy seem scarcely believable in relation to the wild enthusiasm displayed by the fascists not long before – the Allied troops were welcomed by crowds screaming 'Down with Mussolini!', white flag in hand. In Rome the refuse collectors swept Fascist party insignia into the gutter. Hitler never wavered in his attachment to Mussolini, the hero of his youth, but placed the blame on the cowardly and idle Italian people.

In Munich in November 1943 General Jodl gave a memorable address to Nazi party leaders from the various regions of Germany, painting a complete picture of the situation. The text is preserved amongst the documents of the Nuremberg trials and its conclusion is abundantly clear – from then onwards, Germany was on the defensive. Furthermore, Jodl knew that the position could only get worse in the long term, and he said as much: 'The Allied invasion of Europe is now a certainty; we only remain in ignorance of the date and the place.' Jodl's voluminous document is larded with figures relating to every last detail of the strength of the Reich, in terms of men and materials, and lists those of Russia as well. It includes a minute examination of the situation in the war industries. Germany still had 200 divisions (as well as sixteen Romanian and Hungarian divisions): a little over 4 million combatants, of whom 3.9 million were German. But the Soviet Union alone had 378 divisions, including fifty armoured divisions, which comprised 5.5 million men. By 1945 the discrepancy between their respective forces was to reach a Russian superiority of three to one.

Jodl, who was hanged after the Nuremberg trials, was in disgrace with the Führer from time to time, but he remained Chief of the General Staff until the end and his abilities as an officer were never in doubt. None the less, he could find nothing to say to counterbalance the dramatic scenario he had outlined apart from this: 'My most profound reason to remain optimistic is the fact that Germany possesses as her leader a man destined to lead the German people to a brilliant future. . . . My loyalty to the Führer and my faith in him are boundless.' In this he allied himself to Goebbels, the regime's Minister of Propaganda, who proclaimed: 'My weapon is called Adolf Hitler.'

Between the beginning of 1943 and the last days of April 1945, when Gertraüd (Traudl) Junge, *née* Humps, left the bunker in the

the Berlin Reich Chancellery to begin a new life after the double suicide of Hitler and his mistress Eva Braun, she had spent two years and four months in Hitler's immediate entourage. Throughout that time the Führer lived mostly in his headquarters at the Wolfsschanze (the Wolf's Lair) in East Prussia, with brief stays at his famous mountain residence, the Berghof, above Berchtesgaden in Bavaria. He was always surrounded by a small group of colleagues known as the inner circle. During those last years of the Führer's life hardly a day went by, Traudl Junge tells us, when she did not have meals with him or spend long hours working or, more often, relaxing in his company.

At the time she went to work for him as his third and youngest secretary she was a girl of twenty-two, typical of the generation which had grown up in the aftermath of the First World War. Brought up to respect paternal discipline, she had no ideas of her own and no political education. The German woman's universe was still limited to the 'three Ks': *Kinder, Küche und Kirche*, or Children, Kitchen and Church. Because of the retrograde spirit of the phrase it is often attributed to Hitler; in fact it dates from some time earlier, but none the less fits his conception of a woman's role perfectly.

When the war broke out, preceded by the ceaseless trumpeting of propaganda, it meant for Traudl Humps what it meant for thousands of other Germans: a campaign undertaken by a providential leader to redress the injustices of the Treaty of Versailles and restore to Germany her national dignity. The news of the disaster at Stalingrad, just at the time when Traudl Junge joined Hitler's staff, was a rude shock for everybody, and one of Hitler's longest-serving staff, Christa Schroeder, another secretary, said she wept that day. But of course neither she nor her new young colleague knew the contents of Jodl's report. Traudl Junge had no overall view of the military situation. Her secretarial functions gave her no access to the daily briefing sessions, which were exclusively military meetings. According to the statements made by Jodl at Nuremberg, Hitler became more and more suspicious of career officers from 1942 onwards, and began to have his midday meal alone. The daily reports were always made in the presence of a senior SS officer. 'Special stenographers supplied by the Director of the Chancellery [Martin Bormann] took down every word I said,' Jodl testified.

This clarifies the position of Traudl Junge, whose experience was limited to the final period at Hitler's headquarters. The secretaries' workload had been reduced to the point where she steeled herself one day to suggest to the Führer that they might be more useful to the war effort in another capacity. Her duties and those of her colleagues at this time were limited to typing out the Führer's speeches – although he hardly made any by that time – and to courtesy correspondence, letters of congratulations and thanks. Even notes and reports of a political nature were the province of party officials and their colleagues. The chief duties of Hitler's three secretaries, whom the military personnel referred to as 'those ladies', were to appear at his dinner table and to be present at the endless teas during which Hitler tried to relax and forget his worries.

Of course, the fact that the news was becoming more and more disturbing did not escape Traudl Junge, especially when she was called on to type reports on the increasing bombing raids made on Germany. But, in her more modest way, she had the same reaction as General Jodl: 'I thought that a man like the Führer, who had waged war across the whole of Europe for so long, wouldn't continue to act as he did unless he had a solution in sight.' *Der Führer weiss besser* – 'The Führer knows better' – was the dictum that had sustained the vast majority of Germans for many years.

It may seem paradoxical that the staff of Hitler's immediate entourage – his orderly officers, his adjutants and his secretaries – were not the best informed about the progress of events. Ordinary Germans had access to news on foreign radio stations and, as in all dictatorships, an ear to the ground for rumours. But it was obviously inconceivable for anyone to listen to the BBC World Service at the Führer's GHQ, or to spread news gleaned from foreign, and therefore enemy, sources. The optimism of leadership dominated the atmosphere, especially because of the undeniable dynamism that Hitler seemed able to instil in everyone who came near him. There are countless testimonials to his quasi-hypnotic power, even from foreign observers who were far from being admirers of his.

The extermination of the Jews was never mentioned at the Berghof. Of course Hitler's staff, like all Germans, knew of the existence of concentration camps: by the end of the 1930s there were thousands of internees, mainly political prisoners, at camps such as the one at Dachau, near Munich. Most Germans knew of the deportation of Jews and assumed that they were sent to camps similar to the ones in Germany where people were herded together in poor conditions and might even have died of exhaustion and hunger, but were not actually gassed.

The first extermination camps were in operation in December 1941, and specially adapted lorries were being used. There are many reasons why the German public would not have heard of them. On the one hand they were in Poland and other occupied countries from which little news emerged as there were no further military operations there or other contacts. Furthermore, only a small percentage of those killed were German Jews; the millions came from Poland, the USSR, Czechoslovakia, Hungary and the rest of occupied Europe.

'Of course,' says Frau Junge, 'we knew of the existence of the concentration camps, but at our secretarial level we didn't really know what was going on – only that they were terrible camps where starving people had to do hard labour. When one of us made a serious mistake we used to say half-jokingly, "Watch out! You'll be sent to Dachau!" '

We should not expect from Traudl Junge either political revelations or the kind of secret information which has in any case been disclosed in the over-abundant literature on the subject. Most of her long account was written in 1948 soon after Germany's defeat; only the parts concerning her flight from the Chancellery and her adventurous trek across Russian-occupied German territory were recorded in interviews over the course of the last two years. The interest of her story lies in her observation of the details of Hitler's everyday life in the period leading up to his suicide, and the insights into his private personality.

Traudl Junge's account is augmented at times by the recollections of two other members of Hitler's staff – Otto Günsche, one of the Führer's aides-de-camp from 1943 to the end of April 1945, and Hans Baur, his personal pilot. They were present at some occasions when Frau Junge was not, and provide information about the military situation to which she was not privy.

Günsche's recollections of the war and of life in the bunker are typical of a career officer in Hitler's SS. Despite the doubts which assailed him towards the end of the war, an officer's duty is to obey orders at all time and to fight to the last no matter whether he believes in what he's fighting for or not. Hans Baur, on the other hand, was a civilian pilot whom the Führer had requested be released from his job with Lufthansa. He was never involved in any military activities but was responsible for transporting Hitler when he went on propaganda tours, so his relationship with his boss was somewhat less formal than Günsche's.

A book such as this could be criticised for making Hitler seem too human, ceremoniously kissing the hands of his guests and of his secretaries, or spending long hours playing with his favourite dog. One should probably bear in mind that history abounds in examples of infamous tyrants who were capable of equally surprising tenderness. It is generally agreed today that the most shattering feature of those who commit genocide is not that they are monsters, but that they are just like many other people.

In her book *Eichmann in Jerusalem* the Jewish writer and philosopher Hannah Arendt talks of the 'banality of evil'. That is something that stands out clearly in these recollections of some of the witnesses to the last moments of Hitler's Reich.

1

'National Socialism is Dead'

Frau Junge begins her story in Berlin just before the end of Hitler's Third Reich.

By 22 April 1945 an acute sense of anxiety had spread throughout the bunker. Outside, it was like the depths of hell. During the daytime the rumble of gunfire never stopped, and explosions that rocked the ground continued all night long. The Wilhelmplatz was no more than a bomb site and the Kaiserhof palace was a mound of rubble. All that remained of Goebbels's Ministry of Propaganda was a single expanse of white-painted wall, standing alone like a movie set.

Imprisoned in the bunker, we tried to get hold of some news about the outcome of the battle. It should have been at its height. Was that the noise of our guns and tanks? Nobody knew.

Since 16 January, when Hitler had installed himself in his concrete shelter, we had to spend our time inside the bunker: it was our ninety-sixth day spent fifty feet underground, beneath sixteen-feet-thick slabs of cement resting on walls some six feet wide at their base.

The double doors of Hitler's conference room remained shut. Bitter arguments were probably going on in there, but we couldn't hear anything. Eva Braun had taken to her room. The secretaries, Gerda Christian, Else Krueger and I, stayed in the kitchen, where Constanze Manziarly, a young Austrian who had wanted to be a schoolteacher but had become the Führer's private cook because of her skills as a dietician, was getting his meal ready. We drank some very strong black coffee. No one thought about lunch, although the usual time had long since passed. From time to time we could hear the sound of raised voices, then nothing. The Führer was shouting, but we couldn't understand what he was saying. Suddenly Martin Bormann, Director of the Chancellery, burst out of the room in a state of tremendous excitement. He thrust some sheets of paper into the hands of Else Krueger, his secretary: they were to be typed immediately. Glancing quickly through the half-open door, we saw the uniformed backs of the men bent over a vast map of Berlin.

At long last the Führer sent for me, together with Gerda Christian, who had been his secretary since 1934, and Constanze Manziarly. A terrible sense of danger hung in the air. Several officers, their faces as pale as death, stood immobile against the wall of the conference room antechamber. An aide-de-camp led us into Hitler's private apartment, where Eva Braun joined us.

Even before Hitler spoke, we all guessed what he was going to say. He was completely without expression, his face sickly, almost ghost-like. He didn't look at us as he spoke; it was hard to tell if he even saw us.

'Get yourselves ready right away. In one hour's time a plane will take you to the south. It's all over. It's the end. There's no hope left.'

The tone of his voice was quite impersonal; he was simply issuing an order. He was giving up everything. His ability to delude himself, his capacity for wishful thinking, had melted away. Now ironically, it was he who was putting an end to the hope that still flickered in us. Despite everything we felt great pity for him – he was a battered and betrayed man, alone, broken-hearted, thrown abruptly down from his pedestal.

There was a deathly silence for several minutes. We all felt paralysed. The first to come to her senses and break the silence was Eva Braun. Without faltering she walked over to Hitler, took his hands in hers and smiled very sweetly. Gently, as if she were comforting a child, she said, 'You know perfectly well that I'll never leave you. Why are you asking me to go?' Then the Führer did something that even his closest friends had never seen him do. Ignoring us completely, he kissed Eva on the lips.

Suddenly, I felt overwhelmed by guilt. I thought of all the misery that people were suffering throughout the country, so close to us, misery that had lasted for years and for which one man was responsible: Adolf Hitler, our boss. How could I go back home to Munich, to my family and friends? My mother had never liked Hitler. How would she and the others react when I turned up, saying, 'Here I am again! I've made a bad mistake, I

know – but I had the right to save my own neck, didn't I?'
I knew perfectly well that everyone would regard me as
guilty.

A mixture of pity and this sense of culpability pushed me to
see it through to the end. Gerda Christian seemed to be thinking
the same thing because, almost simultaneously, we said, 'We'll
stay in the bunker too.' A few days earlier Magda Goebbels had
already said, 'My husband is *Gauleiter* of Berlin. My children and
I will share his fate.'

Hitler stared at Gerda and myself for a few moments, then
said, 'I order you to leave!'

When we answered 'No!', he took our hands, pressed them
tightly in gratitude and said, 'If only our generals had been as
brave as you!'

Constanze Manziarly now had no reason for staying but said
in turn, 'I won't leave either.'

Hitler went out to the officers who were waiting in the
corridor. 'Gentlemen,' he said, 'the end is approaching. I shall
stay in Berlin and I shall kill myself when the moment comes.
Any of you who wish to leave may do so. You are all free to
go.' Most of the officers left the bunker a little while later.

Back in his bedroom Hitler called his faithful adjutant, Julius
Schaub, and ordered him to burn all the documents stored in a
cupboard in the bunker. Almost overcome by his feelings, Schaub
made three or four journeys up to the garden of the Chancellery,
where he lit a fire and destroyed the papers. Hitler then asked
him to do the same with the documents in Munich and at Berchtesgaden, and that same day Schaub, with tears in his eyes, left
the bunker. The liaison officers went too.

Martin Bormann, Ambassador Walter Hewel, General Hans
Krebs, General Burgdorf, Admiral Voss, General Hermann
Fegelein (who was married to Gretl Braun, Eva's sister), and the
aides-de-camp Nikolaus von Below and Otto Günsche decided
not to go, as did one of the valets, Heinz Linge, and three
orderlies. Several members of the General Staff, telephonists,
drivers and kitchen employees also elected to stay.

The hours passed. I was exhausted and dazed. It was now very
late and I should have gone to bed at least two hours earlier, but
I was eaten up with anguish. If there was any important news, I
didn't want to miss it. I didn't know if the Führer had found a
moment in which to have something to eat. He was closeted in
his bedroom with Goebbels. I wondered what the Propaganda

3

Minister could possibly think of to say to the German people. How would he get out of this mess? How would he react to Hitler's decision to stay in Berlin and to die in the bunker?

At that moment the door opened and Goebbels appeared. He walked to a room where there was a telephone, and when he came back gazed around as if he were looking for someone. He came over to me and said, 'My wife will be arriving with the children. The Führer wants her to stay in the bunker. Could you please make my family welcome, and look after them?'

My God! I thought. Where are we going to put these new arrivals, and what on earth are we going to do with six children? I went up to the first floor to tell Otto Günsche, and he immediately gave orders to have a room that was piled with cases, bags, cardboard boxes and furniture cleared out; the orderlies then filled it with beds for the Goebbels family.

In the meantime, Field Marshal Wilhelm Keitel and General Alfred Jodl were in conference with the Führer. Later on, I overheard by chance a conversation between these two, Martin Bormann and Ambassador Hewel: they were saying that they had tried to persuade Hitler to leave Berlin. There was no longer any reason, they said, to stay in the besieged capital: very soon the different headquarters along the various fronts would all be moving towards the south and it would be impossible for the Führer to communicate with his generals. But their efforts had been in vain. Hitler's resolve was stronger than ever. 'Alive or dead,' he declared, 'I shall not fall into the hands of the enemy. I can no longer fight on the battlefield; I'm not strong enough. I shall kill myself.'

In the last days of April Hitler learned of the atrocious death of his old friend Mussolini, and this had strengthened his resolve to commit suicide. He said, 'At all costs, I must not be taken prisoner. My body must be burned and so well hidden that no one will ever find any remains.'

I am still astonished when I think of the fatalistic calm with which we discussed the most convenient and least painful method of killing ourselves. That day we were at table, in the middle of lunch, when the macabre subject came up again almost without our noticing it.

'The safest way,' Hitler declared, 'is to put the barrel of a revolver in your mouth and pull the trigger. The skull is shattered in pieces and death is instantaneous.'

Eva was horrified by this idea. 'I want to be a beautiful corpse,' she protested. 'I'm going to take poison.' From the pocket of her elegant dress she produced a small capsule in a yellow copper casing. It was cyanide. 'But will it hurt?' she asked. 'I'm terrified of a slow and painful death. I may have made up my mind to die courageously, but at least I want it to be painless.'

Hitler explained to her that death by cyanide poisoning doesn't hurt. 'Death occurs within a matter of minutes. The nervous and respiratory systems are paralysed immediately.'

This explanation prompted Frau Christian and me to ask the Führer to give us each one of the capsules. Heinrich Himmler, the Minister of the Interior and head of the Gestapo, had just brought him a dozen of them. After lunch, Hitler came to us and said, 'Here is a capsule for you, Frau Christian, and one for you, Frau Junge. I am sorry I can't offer you a better farewell present.'

The Goebbels family had just arrived and I went to welcome them. I became responsible for the five little girls and one little boy. Each of the six children had a first name beginning with H, in honour of Hitler: Helga, Holde, Hilde, Heidi, Hedda and Helmut. They were thrilled to see 'Uncle Adolf'. I took them up to the Chancellery, so that they could choose some clothes and toys from among the great variety of presents that had been sent to Hitler on his last birthday, and in a very short time the bunker was filled with their shouts and laughter. They were adorable children, all very well-behaved and quite unspoiled. We knew that their parents, Magda and Joseph Goebbels, had decided to end the children's lives along with their own. Obviously they hadn't the least idea of what was going to happen and I did all I could not to show them how unhappy I was. The children confided to one of the orderlies that they were all going to have an injection so they didn't get sick.

The air raid sirens howled again, very quickly followed by a terrifying bombardment and the noise of the anti-aircraft guns. We were so used to it now that we felt ill-at-ease when the din stopped. Silence had become hard to bear.

Hitler seemed more and more impenetrable. Even after Stalingrad he had never admitted the slightest doubt about the eventual victory; now, with the same conviction, he insisted that the situation was beyond redemption. When someone in his entourage reminded him of Frederick the Great's famous saying 'Whoever throws the last battalion into battle will be the victor,' the Führer screamed, 'The army has betrayed me! My generals are useless!

My orders are never carried out! It's all over! National Socialism is dead and can never be revived! Never!'

We were stunned. We wondered whether we had made the right choice in deciding to stay in Berlin. Perhaps we'd made that decision because deep down we believed we could get out alive. And here was Hitler himself putting an end to those hopes.

He couldn't bear to be alone. He paced up and down the various rooms talking about his imminent death to whoever he happened to meet. Anybody would do. Eva Braun had an obsession about the loyalty of the Führer's former companions. 'I can't understand why they've all deserted you,' she kept saying. 'Where are Himmler, Speer [Minister for Armaments], Ribbentrop [Foreign Minister] and Goering [*Reichsmarschall*, Commander in Chief of the Luftwaffe and Hitler's appointed successor]? Why aren't they at your side, where they ought to be? Where's Brandt [Hitler's former surgeon]?'

Hitler would defend them all, saying, 'You don't understand, my dear child. They're much more use to me where they are. Himmler is in charge of our divisions. Speer has a vital job to do. They've all got essential duties and responsibilities.'

Eva admitted the truth of this. 'But Speer, for example, he's your friend. Your real friend. I'm sure he'll come. I know him.'

During this discussion Himmler telephoned, and the Führer left the room to speak to him. When he came back his face, pale at the best of times, was ashen grey. Once again Himmler had tried to persuade Hitler to leave Berlin, and once again the Führer had absolutely refused. When he told us about this conversation, he repeated his intention of committing suicide. The tone of his voice was quite impersonal, indifferent even, as if he were talking about a normal, logical action. As we listened to him talking about his suicide, we could imagine our own deaths. Little by little we were beginning to get used to the idea.

I couldn't sleep a wink that night. In fact, nobody could sleep any more. We no longer had any clear idea of the date or the time, and life in the bunker had taken on a nightmarish quality.

By 26 April, we were cut off from the outside world apart from a radio link with Field Marshal Keitel. There was not a single word of news about General Wenk's army, or about General Steiner's attack, which was expected to break through the enemy encirclement of Berlin. It began to be obvious that we no longer had an army capable of saving us. The Russians had reached the outskirts of Berlin, and had already made headway into the Tiergarten district. They were meeting little resistance on their march towards the centre of the city and were not even forced to slow their advance as they neared the Anhalt station.

The sound of guns was coming closer and closer, but the atmosphere in the bunker remained the same. Hitler was haggard and absent-minded. After his explosion of temper against his generals the previous day he was hollow-eyed and paler than ever. He seemed completely to have given up his role as leader. There were no briefing sessions, no more fixed schedules, no maps spread out on the table. Doors stood wide open. Nobody bothered with anything any more. Our single obsession was that the moment of Hitler's suicide was approaching.

Goebbels, Werner Naumann, his Secretary of State at the Propaganda Ministry, and Günther Schwägermann, his aide-de-camp, arrived to discuss with Hitler their plans for a final radio broadcast. The population were to be told that the Führer was staying in the besieged capital and that he would personally take part in the city's defence. It was a futile hope that this message would give the German people the courage and energy to achieve the impossible: the sad truth was that there were few able-bodied men left, and a large number of youngsters would sacrifice their lives in vain at a time when their Führer had already given up.

As the Führer wandered like a ghost through the dark labyrinth of the bunker, up and down the silent corridors and into the different rooms, aimlessly, I wondered why he didn't put an end to it there and then. It was obvious that nothing could now be saved. But, at the same time, the thought of his suicide made me feel deeply disappointed that the first soldier of the Reich should do away with himself while children were fighting to defend the capital. I plucked up courage to ask: 'My Führer, don't you think that the German people expect you to put yourself at the head of your troops and to fall in action?'

His reply betrayed the extent of his weariness. 'My hands are trembling so much I can hardly hold my pistol. If I was wounded, none of my men would be prepared to give me the *coup de grâce* – and I don't want to fall into the hands of the Russians.'

He was right. His hands trembled as he lifted his fork to his mouth. He had trouble getting up from his chair. His feet dragged along the ground as he walked.

Despite the atmosphere of despair, the violence and the explosions, the Goebbels children felt safe near 'Uncle Adolf'; they played in the corridors or immersed themselves in books.

At four o'clock they had a cup of chocolate with him, telling him all sorts of stories and gossip about school. Helmut repeated the flattering little speech he had read to 'Uncle Adolf' on his birthday, and his sister Helga protested, 'Helmut, that's the same speech that Daddy made.' Everyone burst out laughing when Helmut answered. 'No, it's not. It was Daddy who copied what *I* said.'

Frau Goebbels and her husband were sleeping in the bedroom of Dr Theo Morell, Hitler's doctor, as he had left Berlin the previous day after a particularly dramatic scene with the Führer. Dr Morell was getting ready to give him his daily injection of a vitamin and hormone cocktail when Hitler, suddenly suspecting a trick, screamed at him: 'Morell, get out of here! Out! You're planning to knock me out and force me to leave Berlin! That's what you all want – but I'm not going!' Morell was devastated, and began to tremble from head to toe when Hitler ordered him to leave Berlin immediately. Never before had Hitler been parted from his beloved Dr Morell, and now he was throwing him out like a leper, a traitor. He no longer wanted his care, his medicines or his special recipes.

New faces began to appear in the bunker. Among them was Artur Axmann, who had succeeded Baldur von Schirach as head of the Hitler Youth when Schirach was appointed *Gauleiter* of Vienna. Axmann had been responsible for printing the first pamphlets and books of Nazi propaganda, including *Mein Kampf.* He had been at Hitler's side during the 'first hours', in the 1920s, and was completely devoted to him. Although he had lost an arm in a hunting accident in 1931, his eyes still shone with the spirit of an old fighter; now he wanted to be close to his Führer during these 'last hours'.

Albert Speer was another new arrival, and Eva Braun was overjoyed. 'I knew you'd come,' she said. 'I always knew you wouldn't abandon the Führer.'

Speer gave a ghost of a smile, then said, after a pause, 'I'm leaving Berlin this evening.'

Eva was writing her letters of farewell. All the dresses she loved so much, her jewels and valuables had already been sent to Munich. She too was suffering from the waiting, but outwardly she showed the same serene resignation as ever. Just once, she came to me and clasped my hands, her voice hoarse and trembling: 'Frau Junge, I'm so frightened. I just want it all to be over!'

Her eyes gave away all the sadness she kept hidden deep inside herself.

Eva was astonished that Hermann Fegelein, her brother-in-law, wasn't giving her any support. She hadn't seen him for two days, and even before that she'd got the impression that he was avoiding her. She asked me if I'd seen him, but he wasn't in the bunker that day. Nobody knew where he was. Perhaps he'd gone on a tour of inspection of the nearest front line? The officers who shared his office in the New Chancellery hadn't seen him either.

On 27 April Hitler sent for Fegelein, but once again he was nowhere to be found. Then the Gestapo took up the search. That night, the SS general was located in his private apartment and arrested, wearing civilian clothes, with none of his medals or the insignia of his rank, and completely drunk. I never saw him again. A very upset and disappointed Eva told me how Fegelein had telephoned her during the night to say: 'Eva, if you can't convince the Führer to get out of Berlin, you must leave without him. Don't be an idiot! It's a question of life and death now.' She asked him where he was, and told him that Hitler wanted to speak to him, but he'd already hung up.

There were no newspapers in Berlin now. We had nothing but the radio, which reiterated over and over again that the Führer was still in the city, sharing its fate and personally directing its defence. Only our little group in the bunker knew that Hitler had long ago withdrawn from the struggle and was simply waiting to die. Opposite, in the Chancellery bunker, the soldiers and the brigade of guards were singing battle songs, while the nurses and the women who had volunteered to help them worked like demons. From all over the city refugees were pouring in, and the men and women of the relief services, who still held out some hope, wanted to do their duty to the end.

The Führer's bunker, by contrast, was like a waxwork museum, but even there there was still some remnant of normal life, a small human touch. It was the sixtieth birthday of a high-ranking SS officer named Rattenhuber, and we all got together to drink his health in the corridor of the upper storey, where chairs and tables were set out for the bunker personnel who took their meals there. Eva Braun was on one side of him; I was on the other. We talked about Bavaria, and how sad it was to die so far from home. 'And surrounded by *Prussians!*' Rattenhuber added, being a typical Bavarian. His eyes abruptly clouded over, but none the less we managed to laugh.

9

Suddenly, a whole crowd of people arrived – some of them familiar faces, others unknown to us. They came from all the neighbouring bunkers. A long line formed, reaching right down to the Führer's bunker, and we saw Hitler moving slowly along it. He held out his hand to each person, looking at them without seeing them. Everyone's eyes shone with pleasure: they were delighted to hear the Führer praising and thanking them, and they went back to their different occupations reassured. But we knew this wasn't Hitler's expression of his gratitude for their courage and their zeal – it was his farewell. 'Has the time come?' I asked Eva Braun. 'No, you'll be warned,' she said. 'The Führer will want to say goodbye to you too.'

That same night there was a wedding: a kitchenmaid married one of the drivers. The bridegroom had somehow managed to bring his fiancée's mother and family through the hell of the city to the Chancellery, and we made our way up through dark passages into a room in the Führer's old apartments, now in ruins and partly lit by candles. It was cold and eerie. There were some rows of chairs and a podium. The Secretary of State, Dr Werner Naumann, gave an address; the couple joined hands to the strains of a horrible organ accompaniment; and we could hardly make out the solemn words as the walls trembled and the windows rattled. As soon as we had congratulated the young couple we hurried back to the bunker of death, but the guests decided to have a party. One produced an accordion, another a violin, and the newly-weds danced together as if they were dancing on the edge of a volcano.

All this time I looked after the Goebbels children, reading them stories or playing games of forfeits with them, trying to keep them as far removed as possible from the horrifying events around us. Their mother couldn't cope with them any longer. At night they slept peacefully in their little beds, while those of us waiting for the end in that bunker felt our fears and anxieties grow.

2

Hitler's Last Will and Testament

On 28 April Hitler suffered one blow after another, as an avalanche of bad news descended on the bunker. The Führer was becoming more and more convinced that he was being betrayed and abandoned by everyone. Just then the Chief Press Officer, Heinz Lorenz, brought him some devastating news: according to a Reuter's report, Himmler was carrying on negotiations with the Allies through the intermediary of the Swedish Count Bernadotte. I can't remember exactly where I was when Hitler got this piece of news. From what I heard later, there was one last mighty explosion of furious shouting, but by the time I saw him he was untypically calm.

Eva Braun was red-eyed with crying because the wayward Hermann Fegelein, her brother-in-law, had been condemned to death: he was shot like a dog in the grounds of the Ministry of Foreign Affairs, amongst the spring flowers. Eva had tried to explain to Hitler that Fegelein, after all, was only obeying his human impulses and thinking of his wife and child in trying to escape to start a new life. But Hitler was immovable: he saw nothing but treachery and deception all around him now. Even Himmler, the 'faithful Heinrich' whom he'd believed to be a paragon of loyalty in the midst of an ocean of cowardice and intrigue, had fallen from grace.

Because of this, Fegelein's own behaviour had taken on a deeper significance in Hitler's mind: he must have been accomplice to a conspiracy. After the revelation of Himmler's secret ambitions, Hitler began to believe that he was plotting another assassination attempt against him – or, worse still, planning to deliver him into the enemy's hands alive. These mad thoughts were fuelled by extreme disappointment as he'd always thought of Himmler as his most devoted collaborator. But now he was suspicious of everyone in Himmler's entourage (and Fegelein had been his liaison officer with the Führer); his suspicions even led him to question the cyanide pills that Himmler had procured for him.

Dr Stumpfegger, one of the doctors who lived in the bunker, was another who had gradually become an object of the Führer's mistrust. Hitler now had him summoned from the operating theatre where he was working round the clock, and we all witnessed the abrupt way he spoke to him as he handed him one of the capsules. Without a pause Stumpfegger led him into a small side room near the toilets where Hitler's favourite dog Blondi was installed with her litter of puppies, born in March. As the doctor bent over the animal a smell of bitter almonds filled the air, and Blondi instantly fell dead. When Hitler turned back towards us, his face was like a death mask. Without a word, he strode off and shut himself in his room.

The bunker shook with the thundering of the Russian artillery bombardment and the air attack. Grenades and bombs exploded without interruption, and that alone was enough to warn us that the enemy would be at the door in a matter of hours. But inside the bunker there was no unusual activity. Most of the country's leaders were assembled, doing nothing but waiting for the Führer's ultimate decision. Even Bormann, always energetic in the extreme, and the methodical Goebbels were sitting about without the smallest task to occupy them. Axmann, Hewel, Voss and the aides-de-camp, the valets and the orderlies awaited some resolution. Hopes of victory had been upheld throughout recent days, but nobody held such illusions any longer. Wenck and Steiner no longer had any armies to save Berlin. It seemed amazing to me that, despite everything, we still ate and drank, slept and found the energy to speak. We did everything like zombies.

Goebbels held long discussions about the disloyalty of his colleagues, and was especially indignant about Goering's behaviour. A vain and indolent man, so arrogant had Goering been about the invincibility of his air force that he had joked about the utter impossibility of the Allies bombing Berlin. 'That man was never really a National Socialist!' Goebbels now declared. 'He could only keep up his position thanks to the Führer, but he's never lived according to the principles and ideals of National Socialism. He's responsible for the collapse of the Luftwaffe and it's because of him that we're sitting in this bunker waiting for defeat.' Everyone now realised that the regime's two top men had lived for years motivated by the same fierce mutual hatred and rivalry. Magda Goebbels joined in her husband's accusations against the *Reichsmarschall*.

As the hours went by, we became completely indifferent to everything. We weren't even waiting for anything to happen any more. We sat about, exchanging an occasional word and smoking. There was a great sense of fatigue, and I felt a huge emptiness inside me. I found a camp bed in a corner somewhere, lay down on it and slept for an hour.

It must have been the middle of the night when I woke up. In the corridors and in the Führer's apartments there was a great deal of coming and going by busy-looking valets and orderlies. I washed my face in cold water, thinking that it must be the moment for the Führer's night-time tea. When I went into his office, he held out his hand to me and asked: 'Have you had some rest, my dear?'

Slightly surprised by the question, I replied, 'Yes, *mein Führer.*'

'Good. It won't be long before I have some dictation for you.'

I wondered what it could possibly be that he wanted to dictate, and as I turned towards a table on which stood eight champagne glasses guests began to arrive: the Goebbels, Gerda Christian, Constanze Manziarly and General Krebs. I was still wondering about the reason for this gathering when Hitler said to me, 'Perhaps we could make a start.'

We left his office and made our way to the conference room. I was just getting ready to type when Hitler said, 'No, take this down in shorthand, on that pad of paper.' And he began immediately: 'This is my political testament. . . .'

For a few seconds my hands trembled. Was I at long last going to hear what I'd waited for: an explanation of all these tragic events, perhaps, or a confession, or an attempt at self-justification? Was the man standing in front of me, the man who'd proclaimed that the Reich would last a thousand years and who had nothing left to lose, at last going to tell the whole truth?

As it turned out, no. Quite calmly, almost automatically, he began to enumerate the accusations, the needs and the demands that I, like every other German, had heard him list a hundred times before. Apart from a short interruption to see to his little group of guests, Hitler continued dictating his so-called political testament in the same vein without a break.

Since the day he had volunteered for the First World War, he began, he had dedicated his thoughts, his actions and his life itself to his people. By the third paragraph, he was claiming never to have wanted the war of 1939, and added that 'it had been wished for and incited by international statesmen of Jewish origin or else acting on behalf of Jewish interests'. A few lines further on, he went back to the same subject: 'Centuries may pass, but from the ruins of our villages and of our great monuments will rise again the eternal, ever-growing hatred for these people who, in the end, must bear the responsibility: the Jews and their acolytes.'

On each of the following sheets of paper, no matter what point he was addressing, he returned to the Jews and their misdeeds. This confirmed, if it were ever necessary, that in the hierarchy of Hitler's hatreds – and there were others, notably the aversion he felt towards the decrepit Hapsburg empire – 'the Jew' (the Nazis used this contemptuous singular) indisputably held first place.

On the other hand, in the scale of his preferences it was England for whom he felt most sympathy. 'After the First World War, that catastrophic war, I never wanted another war against England, nor against the United States.' Hitler recalled the proposals for a solution that he had put to the British Ambassador three days before the invasion of Poland. They included a plan to deal with the German–Polish problem, to be administered under international control. This proposal had failed, Hitler claimed, because of international Jewish propaganda. The next paragraph mentioned 'Jewry' again, as being responsible for the death by starvation of millions of Aryan children in Europe; yet, according to him, the guilty parties had not had to pay for their crimes. Obviously, I thought later, after we had all learned of the plight of the Jews, the holocaust hadn't seemed to him an adequate price.

In the following paragraph Hitler explained the reasons which had made him decide to remain in Berlin during the siege, together with the reasons why he had resolved not to fall into the hands of the enemy for the amusement of the masses: 'a new show . . . stage-managed by the Jews'. He then addressed the brave men and women who had continued the struggle, thanking them and exhorting them to continue to fight to the death.

In the second part of the testament Hitler outlined the practical measures he was taking to appoint his successors as head of the party and of the state. He began by expelling *Reichsmarschall* Hermann Goering from the party and cancelling all the privileges he'd enjoyed as Hitler's appointed successor. In his place, Admiral

Dönitz was named President of the Reich and Supreme Commander of the Wehrmacht. [Admiral Dönitz assumed these functions on 1 May, when he addressed the nation in a radio speech, but he resigned on the 23rd, after Germany's surrender, at the insistence of the Russians. Churchill seemed keen to keep him in the post, in order to have someone in a future German government with whom to communicate, and perhaps out of his preference for naval officers. But Stalin didn't want public recognition of the fact that a German could be anything other than a Nazi.]

In his testament Hitler also expelled Heinrich Himmler from the party, accusing both him and Goering of treason because of the negotiations they had been conducting with the enemy without his knowledge and against his wishes, and because they had tried to seize power, thus inflicting untold harm on the country and the people, quite apart from their personal disloyalty to him.

Hitler named a new government under the Presidency of Dr Goebbels, as Chancellor of the Reich, with a restricted number of ministers (eleven in all). Among these, Dönitz would be Minister of War, the Ministry of Foreign Affairs would be held by the Austrian Seyss-Inquart, the Reich's Commissioner for Holland, and the Finance Ministry by Count von Schwerin-Krosigk. He went so far as to name the holders of the portfolios of Agriculture, Education and Employment, but these people never had time to take up their posts.

Then he interrupted his dictation for a moment to say: 'Now I'm going to dictate my own last wishes, my personal will.

'During the years of combat, I was unable to commit myself to a contract of marriage, so I have decided, this day, before the end of my earthly life, to take as my wife the young woman who, after many years of faithful friendship, has of her own free will come to the besieged capital to link her fate to my own. She will, according to her own wishes, go to her death as my wife. For us, this will take the place of all that was denied us by my devotion to the service of my people.

'Everything of any value I possess I bequeath to the party, or, if it no longer exists, to the state. If the state itself is wiped out, no decision of mine is of any consequence.

'The pictures I have collected [STOLEN FROM ALL OVER EUROPE] over the course of years have never been acquired in the spirit of personal gain, but with the

15

intention of donating them to a gallery in my home town of Linz, on the Danube.

'I hope with all my heart that these bequests will be executed.'

That was how I learned that he was going to marry Eva Braun.

The dictation was over. He left the table on which he'd been leaning throughout, as if he needed a support, and suddenly his face showed immense fatigue. His voice, however, had betrayed impatience, and I realised that this piece of dictation would remain just as he had spoken it, without any revision. I thought of what it had been like when I started to work for him in 1943. Then he was so fussy that the simplest letter of congratulation to a *Gauleiter*, an artist or any minor official was meticulously revised and corrected. But Hitler had no time to spare now.

Suddenly, Goebbels appeared in the antechamber where I was working. I looked at him in astonishment. He was as white as a sheet, and the tears pouring down his cheeks showed the state of high emotion he was in. He wanted to talk to me, probably because there was no one else he could speak to. 'The Führer has ordered me to leave Berlin, Frau Junge, because he's allocated me an important job in the future government. But I don't want to run away, and to leave the Führer. I am the *Gauleiter* of Berlin and my place is here. If the Führer dies, my life has no meaning. He even said to me: "Goebbels, I didn't expect this from you! You refuse to obey my last orders . . . !" ' Goebbels spoke like a broken man, his face bathed in tears. 'The Führer has thought of lots of solutions when it was too late, but this one has come too early. . . .'

Then he too dictated his will, which was to be added to Hitler's as an appendix. He said that he was disobeying his Führer for the first time ever, but that he couldn't abandon his post in Berlin at the Führer's side. In the world to come, an example of loyalty would have more value than one life saved. And he announced to the German people that he preferred to die, together with all his family, than to live in a Germany without National Socialism.

I typed out Hitler's two texts as fast as I could. My fingers worked mechanically. Bormann, Goebbels and the Führer kept coming into the room to find out whether I'd finished: they made me nervous and only held up the work. In the end they practically ripped the last sheets of paper from the typewriter, and carried them back to the conference room where the three copies were signed and dispatched by courier to different destinations. The couriers were Colonel von Below, Heinz Lorenz and Zander, one of Bormann's assistants, who had taken on the task of getting Hitler's last wishes out of Berlin.

With this act, the Führer's political life was definitively over. Now, all he had to do was wait for confirmation that at least one of the copies had reached its destination. Those last hours were terrible. We were expecting the Russians to attack the bunker at any moment. The sounds of the battle were getting closer and closer. All our dogs had been given lethal injections.

While I was working on the wills, the marriage ceremony had taken place. My typing completed, I joined the party. We all sat round the table, filled our glasses with champagne and then stood up and raised our glasses to Eva and Adolf. Not a word was spoken. How could we toast the future of the bride and groom?

Otto Günsche, then one of the Führer's aides, has provided this description of the wedding of Hitler and Eva Braun on the night of 28–29 April.

When one speaks of the wedding ceremony of Hitler and Eva Braun, one tends to imagine a relatively cheerful occasion, but the circumstances and the atmosphere in which it took place should be taken into account. It was a union of two people in extremis, both of whom had already made an irrevocable decision to take their own lives the very next day. People have said that a room was specially arranged for the ceremony in an attempt to relieve the sinister decor of the bunker, but in fact nothing was done beyond moving into a small map room a table for the signing of documents and a few seats for the people present. A senior party functionary, a regional party inspector called Walter Wagner, had been brought across Berlin under incessant fire and at great danger to his life: as he had an honorary post in the Berlin city administration, he could serve as a registrar of marriages.

Apart from the couple themselves, the only people present were Goebbels and Bormann, who acted as witnesses to the marriage document, a standard form of two typed pages. The formalities had been reduced to a minimum: the basic question put first to the Führer – 'Adolf Hitler, do you take Eva Braun to be your wife?' – then to the future Frau Hitler. There was another ritual question at the time, about the Aryan origins of the future spouses and the absence of any hereditary diseases, but this question does not seem to have been put to them: no one has been able to ask the people who were present, since they didn't survive, but in any case the question formed part of the preliminaries to the marriage itself.

The newly-weds signed the marriage document, followed by the two witnesses and the registrar. When she was signing her name, Eva began to write the letter B for Braun until Walter Wagner smilingly pointed out her mistake. She crossed it out and signed herself Eva Hitler, *née* Braun, and this correction is clearly visible on the document, which has been preserved.

Straight after signing, Hitler and his wife retired and the two witnesses rejoined those people who were waiting in an ante-chamber. They were Goebbels and his wife, Martin Bormann, the SS General Wilhelm Burgdorf, Ambassador Hewel, the head of the Hitler Youth, Axmann, Colonel Nikolaus von Below, Gerda Christian, one of Hitler's secretaries and Linge, the valet. The wedding feast consisted of a few glasses of champagne and some sandwiches.

An hour and a half later, Eva appeared alone and shook hands with everyone present, all of whom expressed their congratulations. She was smiling and very relaxed. I had been busy with the preparations for the macabre mission the Führer had entrusted me with – making arrangements for the disposal of his and his new wife's bodies – and when I came back into the antechamber I gathered that the wedding had already taken place. When I congratulated her I addressed Eva in the usual way – *Gnädiges Fräulein* – but she interrupted me with a smile: 'You can simply call me "Frau Hitler" now.' In the meantime, other inhabitants of the bunker had appeared to express their congratulations. Hitler himself didn't appear until later, about 2 a.m., because he was in the process of dictating his two wills to Traudl Junge.

Hans Baur, one of Hitler's pilots, was one of the many who tried to persuade Hitler to leave the city.

At about seven o'clock on the evening of 29 April I went to see Hitler. As he was saying goodbye to me, I took the opportunity of telling him once again that I could get him out of Berlin and take him not just to his Bavarian hide-out but anywhere in the world. At the time I had at my disposal a prototype six-engine Junkers with a range of over 6000 miles. We could have gone to any Middle Eastern country well disposed towards the Führer.

But he declined. 'What would be the use? In a few weeks I'd be in exactly the same situation.' He thought, quite rightly, that in his position the only outcome – not just the only possible outcome, but the only desirable outcome – was death.

It was then that Hitler told me of his decision to kill himself. He added that Eva Braun had decided to do the same, although he had asked her not to. 'You must make absolutely sure that both our bodies are burned,' he said. 'Admiral Dönitz is to succeed me as head of state. I've entrusted the act of nomination to Bormann, together with certain other documents, such as the list of the new government with Dr Goebbels as Chancellor and Arthur Seyss-Inquart as Minister of Foreign Affairs. You must get out of Berlin and make sure that Bormann manages to reach Dönitz.'

During this farewell visit, Hitler made me a gift of a picture he was greatly attached to. 'I want to give you that picture hanging on the wall there,' he said. 'It's a portrait of Frederick the Great by Anton Graf. It cost 34,000 marks in 1934. Many of my pictures are much more valuable, but I'm very fond of that one and I don't want it to be lost.' I replied that I'd take it so that I could place it in a museum or gallery later on, but Hitler said, 'It's supposed to be for you. It's enough that you keep it in your possession.' It was indeed a very special picture for Hitler: everywhere he went, even for a brief stay, he immediately had it hung on the wall of his office.

The Führer's last words to me were: 'One must have the courage to face the consequences. Fate wanted it this way. Baur,' he continued, 'I want my epitaph to be "He was the victim of his generals." ' That was the last time I saw him.

3

The Suicide Pact

Frau Junge takes up the story again.

April 30 began like all the days that had preceded it. The hours went by very slowly. We lunched with Hitler, and the conversation at table was the same as the day before and the day before that, and for days past. A death feast, masked by an appearance of calm and serenity.

When we got up from the table, Eva Braun went to her bedroom. My colleague Gerda Christian and I went off to look for a quiet corner where we could smoke a cigarette. I found an empty chair in the valets' room, by the open door to the passage leading to Hitler's apartments. I supposed he must be in his room, but I didn't know who was with him.

After a short time Otto Günsche appeared. 'Come on,' he said. 'The Führer wants to say goodbye.' Fräulein Manziarly, Frau Christian and I got up and walked into the corridor.

The Führer looked more stooped than ever as he came out of his room and moved slowly towards us. He offered his hand to each of us, and as he shook hands he looked straight at me, but I knew he didn't see me. His right hand was warm. He seemed to be a thousand miles away. He whispered some words that I couldn't make out: I've never known what his last words to us were.

The moment we'd all been expecting had finally arrived, but I felt frozen, as if in a trance, understanding nothing of what was happening around me. It was only when Eva Braun came up to me that I came to my senses. She was wearing Hitler's favourite dress, the black one with pink roses at either side of a low square

20

neckline. Her hair was beautifully done. She smiled at me, and put her arm around my shoulder.

'Please try to get out of here,' she said. 'You might make it.' Then she added, 'Give my love to Bavaria!' She smiled again and seemed to choke back a sob.

Then she turned and went with the Führer into his room, to her death. The heavy iron door swung shut behind them.

Shortly before, she had invited me into her bedroom and gone over to one of her cupboards. She had taken out a superb silver fox coat, which she loved. 'Frau Junge,' she had said, 'this is my farewell present to you. I've always enjoyed seeing well-dressed women around me, and now I want you to wear this and enjoy it.'

I had thanked her warmly, though I hadn't the least idea when or where I could possibly wear it. I had noticed her initials, EB, embroidered on the lining, intertwined in the shape of a four-leaf clover. The superstitious Eva had believed it would bring her good luck.

Suddenly, after the door shut behind the two of them, I was seized by a wild desire to get as far away as possible. I almost flew up the steps that led to the upper part of the bunker. But halfway up I remembered the six Goebbels children, abandoned down there: nobody had even thought to give them anything to eat at lunchtime, and they were wandering about looking for their parents or for Aunt Eva. I led them all to the big round table.

'Come on, children, I'll get you some lunch. The grown-ups have all got so much to do today that they haven't had time,' I said as calmly as I could.

I found some fruit and ham and made sandwiches for them, and as they ate I chatted and they answered me cheerfully. They were talking about the safety of the bunker. It was almost as if they were enjoying the constant bombardment and the explosions outside, so certain were they of being out of reach. Suddenly a shot rang out, so close that it silenced us all. The sound echoed round the bunker. 'Right on target!' yelled little Helmut, without any idea of how accurate he was.

Otto Günsche describes the scene that met his eyes as he carried out Hitler's last instructions to him.

When the door to the Führer's apartment closed, there was a

moment's silence. Hitler had stood back to let Eva go through first. I was busy giving instructions to the men and officers who were to carry the two bodies outside. Hitler had told me to wait ten minutes before entering the apartment. They were the longest minutes of my life. I stood by the door like a sentry. Suddenly Magda Goebbels came rushing towards me, as if to force her way through. I couldn't push her back, so I opened the door to ask Hitler what I should do. She practically knocked me over in her desire to get into the room, but she came out again immediately. Hitler hadn't wanted to listen to her and she left sobbing. A moment later Axmann, the head of the Hitler Youth, arrived. This time I was firm and told him: 'Too late!'

Ten minutes later, after hearing the shot, I went into the room. Hitler's body was crumpled up, his head hanging towards the floor. Blood was running from his right temple onto the carpet. The pistol had fallen to the ground. Eva, who was sitting in the other corner of the sofa, her legs curled under her, had stayed in the same position. She showed no trace of any wound. Her pistol was beside her. A vase of flowers had fallen to the floor.

I was frozen, turned to stone. When I finally came to my senses, I had the table and chairs cleared out of the way and blankets spread out on the floor. Several guards had arrived by now, and three of them took Hitler's body, wrapped it in a blanket, and carried it away. Martin Bormann lifted Eva's body, then I took it from him and gave it to the guards. While they were going upstairs, Kempka, the chauffeur, arrived with some men; they had brought about forty gallons of petrol in jerrycans.

The deaths of Hitler and Eva took place about 3.30 p.m. The two bodies were placed in a trench and guards doused them with petrol. We managed to light the fire by throwing pieces of flaming paper into the trench. Suddenly, as the flames shot up, all the men present, without any prior consultation, raised their arms in a Nazi salute.

Frau Junge recalls her thoughts and emotions at this moment.

Now that Hitler was dead, I needed to be alone. The Goebbels children went happily off to their rooms, and I sat on the narrow bench beside the round table. There was a bottle of Steinhaeger schnapps and a glass next to it, which I filled and drank straight down. It really was the end.

I don't know how long I sat there. I heard the sound of boots on the stairs, and men passed close to me without my seeing them, although I did notice the large silhouette of Günsche going by, followed by a strong smell of petrol. His face was ashen and his features so pinched he seemed to have become an old man. He came and dropped heavily onto the seat beside me, grabbing the bottle. His big hands were trembling. 'I've carried out the Führer's last orders . . . I've burnt his body,' he said quietly. I didn't reply. I didn't ask anything.

He went back upstairs to see whether the bodies were completely burnt. I stayed there a moment longer, trying to think what might happen next. Something drew me downstairs again towards the empty bedrooms. In the deepest part of the bunker, at the far end of the corridor, the doors of the two rooms still stood open. The people carrying the bodies probably didn't have a hand free to shut them with.

On a side table stood Eva's little revolver, beside a square of pink silk chiffon. I saw the cyanide capsule of yellow metal on the floor beside her armchair. It looked like an empty lipstick tube. Spread over the armchair, which was upholstered in a blue and white patterned fabric, was a large bloodstain. It was Hitler's blood. A feeling of nausea came over me. I couldn't stand the heavy smell of bitter almonds from the poison. My hand automatically reached for my own cyanide capsule: I wanted to throw it as far as I could and get out of this horrible place immediately. I wanted to breathe fresh air, feel the wind on my face, hear the trees rustling. But freedom, calm and peace were out of reach.

Suddenly, I felt a sort of hatred for the dead Führer, an impotent fury rising up inside me. I hadn't been taken by surprise, because I knew perfectly well he was going to abandon us, but I hadn't imagined this feeling of emptiness and confusion. . . . He had simply gone, and with him the magnetic impulse that had linked us to life itself.

I heard footsteps in the corridor leading to the entrance. The last faithful servants of the Reich, who'd taken part in the incineration of the bodies, were coming back: Goebbels, Bormann, Axmann, Hewel, Günsche and the chauffeur, Kempka. I didn't want to see anyone and I walked quickly away, down the passage cluttered with rubble and debris that led towards my quarters in the neighbouring New Chancellery bunker.

By now a number of other women had moved in there, secretaries from the aides-de-camp's offices whom I already knew. They weren't yet aware of what had happened in the bunker opposite; they were talking about holding the fort, about bravery, laughing and working as if there was still some point in doing so. My suitcases, in which were packed all my things, my books and wedding presents, were still there. I'd wanted them to be somewhere safe, somewhere I could pick them up at any moment, but now they seemed not to belong to me. I wouldn't be able to take anything with me. I threw myself down onto my camp bed and shut my eyes, trying to think about what I had to do, but almost straightaway I fell into a deep sleep.

I woke later that night, just as my friends were getting ready to go to bed and get a few hours' sleep. They still didn't know that Hitler was dead. I didn't want to speak to anyone and I went back over to the Führer's bunker, where I found the whole group of people who had decided to stay in Berlin to the end. Suddenly, these were people who were able to think and act autonomously again, and they were sitting discussing what they should do. Frau Christian and Fräulein Krueger, Bormann's secretary, were also there, and so was little Fraülein Manziarly, her eyes awash with tears. She had cooked Hitler's meals that 30 April, just like any other day, so that no change in the daily routine would arouse the suspicions of anyone who wasn't in on the secret. She'd prepared his usual two fried eggs with mashed potato.

All that was left of Hitler's inner circle was there, and we tried to establish a plan. General Krebs was to present himself to the Soviet general staff and offer the surrender of the troops in Berlin on condition that those in the bunker received a safe-conduct across the occupied capital. He was the highest-ranking officer, and he'd been military attaché in Moscow and spoke Russian. With one officer accompanying him he set off into the night, unarmed, with an improvised white flag. We all waited, drinking coffee and schnapps; everything we said seemed empty of meaning. I could only think of one thing: I had to get out of there. I couldn't let the Russians arrive and find my corpse in that rat trap.

Meanwhile, General Mohnke and Otto Günsche were in the process of forming an escape plan – to team up with some of the soldiers from the bunker and try to find a way across the city. Rationally, there didn't seem to be the slightest chance of getting through alive, but it was better than committing suicide in that hole. Without thinking, Frau Christian and I cried in unison, 'Take us with you!' The two men were friendly to us and nodded their agreement. All we had to do was to wait for the answer Krebs would bring back.

We waited several hours. It was already 1 May, the great national festival. Hitler hadn't wanted to wait. Perhaps he thought it was a date which the Russians would want to celebrate with an all-out attack on the Reich Chancellery; however, the bombardment that day was no worse than it had been for the last several days.

At long last Krebs appeared, exhausted, his expression bleak. We scarcely needed to ask him what news he'd brought: his proposal had been rejected, and we were to prepare ourselves for the breakthrough attack. Just at that moment, Goebbels announced over the radio that the Führer had died in Berlin 'at the head of his troops'.

Now that all the other inhabitants of the bunker knew, there was suddenly a sense of feverish activity. The depots were emptied of supplies accumulated by the commissariat, but there were hardly enough takers for the quantities of jam, wine, champagne, schnapps and chocolate. Under the circumstances, none of that held any great attraction: we were concerned with saving our lives.

General Mohnke gave out weapons to everyone. Even the women were issued with pistols, but advised not to use them except in the direst emergencies. We were also supposed to be given more suitable clothes for our escape, for which purpose we had to go to a depot in a bunker beneath the Vosstrasse, some way away. To get there, we had to pass through the operating room of the medical centre. I had never seen a dead body, and I'd always hated the sight of blood, but that day I saw the horribly disfigured corpses of two soldiers lying on stretchers. Professor Haase didn't even glance up as we passed him: he was busy amputating a leg.

At the depot I was given a tin hat, a pair of trousers, a short jacket and a pair of heavy shoes that I put on after checking the size. Then I went quickly back to our bunker. The strange new clothes seemed to hang off me, and I felt peculiar. Even the men had made changes to their clothing: many of them had taken off their medals and insignia of rank. Captain Hans Baur, Hitler's personal pilot, was rolling up the portrait of Frederick the Great which Hitler used to take everywhere with him and hang in each of his different offices, and which he'd given Baur as a memento on the eve of his death. Ambassador Hewel was his usual indecisive self. He didn't know what choice to make – he was tempted by the idea of killing himself with cyanide, but decided in the end to join our group. (In fact he shot himself in Berlin immediately after getting out of the bunker; he was forty-one.) Our group was also joined by Admiral Voss, Bormann, Naumann, the chauffeur Kempka, Hans Baur and Schwägermann. Everyone now wanted to try to escape.

Suddenly I thought about the Goebbels children. Magda, their mother, hadn't been seen since the night before, when she had shut herself in her room. I wondered if the children were still with her. One of the kitchenmaids, or perhaps one of the housekeepers, had offered to take them with her out of Berlin, saying that the Russians would probably let them all through, but I didn't know whether Frau Goebbels had accepted the offer.

We were sitting about waiting for nightfall. Until that moment the only person who had chosen to commit suicide was Franz Schaedle, head of Hitler's bodyguard, who had been wounded. Abruptly, the door which led towards the Goebbels' apartment opened and a nurse and a man in a white uniform appeared, dragging a huge wooden chest which seemed very heavy. It was followed by a second one and I immediately thought of the six children: it could have been them. I'd thought my heart had hardened to all grief, but I felt a sob rising in my throat.

Then General Krebs and General Burgdorf got up, straightened their tunics and held out their hand to each of us in turn. They didn't want to run away; they preferred to kill themselves there. The rest of us were still waiting for darkness to fall, so that we could attempt to leave. Goebbels came and went, chain smoking. He looked like a restaurateur silently waiting for the last late guests to leave. He wasn't shouting now, or wallowing in self-reproach, as he had done earlier. After a while, the hour seemed to have struck for him too. We all shook him by the hand and said goodbye; with a forced smile on his face, he wished us good luck. 'Perhaps you'll manage to get through,' he said gently. I shook my head. We were already completely surrounded by the enemy, and Russian tanks were in the Potsdamerplatz.

One after the other we left that horrifying place. For the last time I passed the door to Hitler and Eva's apartments. His grey greatcoat was still hanging on a metal coat-rack; above it were his cap with the gold insignia and his leather gloves. The dog's lead was there, hanging like a noose from a gallows. For a second I thought of taking the gloves, or at least one of them, as a memento, but I gave up the idea before I'd even stretched out my hand. I don't really know why. In Eva's bedroom the wardrobe doors stood open, and I caught sight of the silver fox fur coat she'd given me. But what could I have done with a coat like that in a city in the hands of the enemy? I was more likely to need my poison capsule.

We made our way to the huge coal cellar of the New Chancellery. Otto Günsche guided us through the maze of narrow passages. There were four women in the group – Gerda Christian, Else Krueger, Constanze Manziarly and me – and Günsche ushered us through the middle of a band of soldiers ready for action, amongst whom we spotted the familiar faces of Bormann, Baur, Stumpfegger, Rattenhuber and others. Everyone was wearing a tin hat. We all exchanged greetings: for many of us, they were the last.

4

Invitation to the Wolf's Lair

Frau Junge looks back to the time when she first went to work for Hitler.

I would never have become Hitler's secretary if I hadn't had a burning ambition to be a ballerina. From an early age, my younger sister Inge and I had taken dancing and gymnastics lessons in our native Munich, and I had no doubt that one day I'd devote my life to one of these two activities. Unfortunately we were living in difficult financial circumstances, and, being the eldest, I had to take on responsibilities that were in those days not demanded of younger members of one's family. I had to think about getting a job that would allow me to earn my own living as soon as I'd left school. I imagined – naïvely – that if I got a job in a bank I'd be able to earn enough to train as a dancer at the same time. But, in practice, I quickly realised that it wasn't easy to find work which would given me enough to live on and leave me enough time to satisfy my artistic leanings as well. I hoped to work for just as long as necessary to save some money and take the entrance exam to the training school of my choice; then I could abandon the world of the typewriter for the world of dance.

At that point the war broke out, and everyone began to feel the weight of duty and personal restrictions. It was brought home to me that I'd built up my private plans without taking external circumstances into account. In 1941, when at last I managed to pass my exams as a dancer and thought I could tell my employer that I was leaving, people were no longer free to choose their jobs. There was greater need for secretaries and shorthand typists than for ballerinas. I was already twenty-one, and the war looked as if it was going to be a long-term business, not just a brief skirmish.

My disappointment prevented me from looking at things objectively, I suppose, and I directed all my animosity against my boss, whom I held responsible for the failure of my life because, as he was legally entitled to, he had refused to let me leave my job. In the end, though, my stubbornness led me to make another dream come true: to go to Berlin. In the process I set in motion the avalanche that, a few years later, in 1945, almost engulfed me.

My sister Inge lived in the capital, where she had become a dancer at the Deutsche Tanzbühne, the Ballet Theatre. One of her best friends there was the sister-in-law of Albert Bormann, the brother of the Reichsleiter Martin Bormann, one of the most senior officials in the Nazi party. Thanks to her, I heard that a secretarial job in the Chancellery was vacant. I was thrilled at the thought of going to Berlin and beginning a new life. The conditions of work, as they'd been described to me, seemed very appealing and I decided to leave for Berlin straightaway.

Even the train journey in a sleeping car was a great event for me. The following morning, when I was supposed to present myself at the New Chancellery, I got lost in the labyrinth of magnificent hallways, galleries and rooms with marble-inlaid walls, and I started to wonder how I'd adapt to this grandiose environment. My hasty decision began to seem ill considered – but there was no going back.

I was welcomed by Gruppenführer Albert Bormann, who was a pleasant man, easy-going, well educated and unpretentious. As well as being responsible for the management of the Führer's offices in the Chancellery, Bormann was one of his aides-de-camp, so he was seldom in Berlin.

From the start my job consisted of reading and sorting the private letters addressed to the Führer, and passing each one to the appropriate department. The work was straightforward and unchallenging, and I often wondered why they had taken the trouble to bring a girl from Munich to do a simple secretarial job in this vast edifice. My daily life was devoid of surprises at first, but quite soon news arrived to interrupt the routine. It was November 1942. A rumour spread through the offices that Hitler needed a new personal secretary, and that the choice would be made from among the Chancellery staff. Courses and tests in shorthand typing were arranged, and then a preliminary selection was made: I was among the nine girls shortlisted for the job. We were sent by special train to Rastenburg in East Prussia, where the Führer's headquarters – the Wolfsschanze or Wolf's Lair – were located.

At the time Hitler had three secretaries, of whom the youngest, Frau Gerda Christian, had just got married and left his service. The other two, Fräulein Johanna Wolf and Fräulein Christa Schroeder, had been his secretaries for the last ten years. The stresses of such an irregular life, and perhaps also their age, had reduced their ability to cope with the work, but in any case two secretaries were not enough to ensure that the Führer had someone at his disposal every moment of the day and night. Once, when Hitler wanted urgently to dictate something, Fräulein Wolf was sick and Fräulein Schroeder turned out to be in Berlin, at the theatre. Hitler threw himself into a furious rage, shouting and screaming that it was unthinkable that no one should be available when he wanted to work. His aide-de-camp Albert Bormann spent a very unpleasant few minutes. He was ordered to take immediate steps to see that such a thing never happened again, and at the same time to take on new secretaries so that the two older women could be relieved of some of their workload and could train some replacements. That is how, during the last days of November 1942, nine young women received orders to present themselves to the Supreme Commander of Military Forces.

The train we boarded in Berlin one evening carried no indication of its destination, but the next morning we arrived at Rastenburg. We waited in a siding for a light locomotive that took us through the forest to a small, unmarked station where Albert Bormann was waiting to welcome us. A few other passengers got out and disappeared down snow-covered paths that led away from the track, but we continued our journey. There wasn't a house or a building of any kind in sight; none the less, Bormann assured us that we were within the boundaries of the Führer's headquarters, although not yet inside the restricted central zone. On the track beside us stood another train: that was where we were to be lodged for the time being, while waiting for our interviews with the Führer.

This train turned out to be as well appointed as a comfortable hotel, with all the necessary conveniences and furnishings. Each of us slept in a special guest compartment, and we were well looked after by staff trained on the international railway service.

We felt impatient for the great event – our meeting with the Führer – but several days went by and nothing happened, so we started to go out for short walks in the forest around us. We went a little further each time, until one day we found ourselves facing a barbed wire enclosure and an armed guard who demanded our permits and the password. Of course we hadn't any papers, and we had no idea what the password might be; embarrassed, we explained that we were just stretching our legs, hoping to see what the Führer's GHQ looked like, but with no intention of trespassing on forbidden territory. However, we'd had time to catch a glimpse of a large number of wooden barracks and small bunkers hidden among the trees and bushes, linked by well-kept paths through the forest, and we realised that a huge number of uniformed men must live there.

The marvellous winter landscape and, above all, the excellent food we were served gave our stay a holiday atmosphere. We decided to stop worrying about why we were there, and to make the most of it. A small cupboard in the restaurant compartment contained some excellent bottles, and the maître d'hôtel, who hadn't had a chance to look after a party of ladies for a long time, spoiled us with liqueurs in the evenings.

We hadn't guessed that the great moment would come when we were least expecting it, in the middle of the night. We were all in bed when two orderlies from the Führer's bunker arrived to take us to see Hitler. There was complete panic. We all rushed to do our hair, find our shoes from under our beds, our fingers trembled, we could hardly button our clothes. Those of us who smoked had to scrub their teeth, because 'the German woman' was supposed to loathe tobacco.

Finally we set off along the dark paths through the forest, led by the orderlies. It was hard to make out how these two men could find their way in the darkness, using only the occasional flash of a pocket torch, but they got us safely to the guard post where, by the light of a lantern, we were issued with temporary passes for the first restricted zone.

None of us had ever seen Hitler close to, but we knew that wherever he appeared, in Berlin and elsewhere, millions of people rushed to catch even a glimpse of him from a distance. It was thrilling to think that we would be face to face with the head of state. After some time we came to a heavy metal door beneath which we could see a thin strip of light. In the darkness, I could just make out the contours of a very large, low bunker. The armed guard standing at the entrance let us in without checking us in any way; not even our fairly voluminous handbags were searched. It was obvious that they didn't suspect us of carrying weapons or a bomb, and certainly our frightened faces should have allayed any such suspicions, because we must have looked more like victims on their way to execution than terrorists on a murder mission.

After passing through a low door, we found ourselves in a narrow concrete corridor, very brightly lit, rather like a passage on board a large ocean liner, with several doors on either side. We went through the first door on the left, into a waiting room. It was a room about twelve by sixteen feet where Hitler's orderlies and personal valets spent their time. The valet on duty warned us that we'd have to wait a while because Hitler was in the middle of feeding his dog, Blondi. He invited us to sit down on comfortable rustic seats around a circular table.

We asked the valet how we ought to greet the Führer. 'Hitler will probably greet you first,' he replied, 'and you should answer *"Heil, mein Führer!"'.* We wanted to ask him if we should also give the National Socialist salute, with the hand held out or simply raised, but just then Albert Bormann appeared and asked us to follow him, saying that Hitler was back in his office and ready to see us. 'Don't be nervous,' he said. 'Just behave as naturally as possible.'

A narrow passage with a detour through a little tea room led to the high double doors of Hitler's office. The valet, Heinz Linge, knocked at the door, opened it and announced, 'The ladies from Berlin are here, *mein Führer.'* We walked into a large room and found ourselves opposite Hitler's desk. He smiled, slowly raised his arm in a salute, then walked towards us and shook hands. In a calm voice, he asked each of us in turn her name and where she came from. I was the last, and the only one from Munich. He asked how old I was, smiled again, turned on us his famous penetrating gaze, raised his arm in salute once more, and that was that. We had been dismissed without having a chance to blurt out the 'Heil, mein Führer!' we had rehearsed so carefully.

As soon as we were outside the door the tension evaporated, to be immediately replaced by an excited babble of comment about the Führer, his fascinating eyes, his handshake, his way of carrying himself and all the other details of this memorable encounter. Bormann seemed content to have fulfilled his mission. He offered us a glass of champagne, then took us to the nearby camp mess hall, where the soldiers and officers were delighted to see us. We were served sandwiches – the excitement had given us an appetite – then taken back to our special train.

The next day, lengthy discussions about our chances of being chosen began again. We were puzzled about the interview, since we didn't think a secretary could possibly be employed on the basis of such a brief meeting, but Bormann soon informed us that it wouldn't be quite so simple. We were to take a dictation test; once again, it was just a question of waiting. Several of the train staff and various soldiers from the restricted zone used to visit us in the train, and one of them told me he thought I had a strong chance of being chosen. 'The Führer has a soft spot for girls from Munich,' he said, 'and he'd like your accent much more than a Prussian voice. Besides,' he added, with a wink, 'you look a lot like Eva Braun.'

The few days we'd been supposed to spend at the Wolfsschanze turned into weeks, and we still had no idea when Hitler would find the time to call us for a dictation test. From time to time we were asked to help the two older secretaries: for example, when they were drawing up the Führer's Christmas card list. Even so, we had plenty of time to make snowmen – which were destroyed the next day by the GHQ's commandant, who considered them inappropriate to the military surroundings – and to have furious snowball fights with each other. It was just after one of these battles, when my hair was wet and I was still out of breath, that an aide-de-camp arrived to summon me to see Hitler, together with another of the secretaries, a slim, blonde girl called Fräulein Böttcher. Tramping along the path towards the Führer's bunker, we felt excited all over again. On arrival we were told that I was to go in first, and Fräulein Böttcher was to take over from me if things didn't go well.

After a brief wait, I was shown into Hitler's study by Linge. The door closed behind me and I found myself alone with the Führer. The first thing I noticed was that he was wearing a pair of very ordinary old-fashioned glasses with steel rims – although they might have been platinum, because I was later told that he was fond of luxurious materials even for everyday objects. He shook my hand and led me to a small table with a typewriter on it next to his desk. While I took off the cover and put a piece of paper in the machine, he talked to me in a kindly way, as if I were a child about to have her photograph taken. 'There's no need to be nervous. I make a lot of mistakes when I'm dictating – many more than you will, I'm sure.'

I tried to tell him that I wasn't at all nervous, but my hands gave me away: when I finally started to type the first sentence, my fingers trembled so much that I could scarcely hit the keys. I was horrified when I saw my first line – it looked like Chinese – and I had to make a superhuman effort to control my hands. Just at that moment, thank goodness, there was a knock at the door and Ambassador Hewel, who was responsible for liaison between the Führer and the Ministry of Foreign Affairs, was shown into the room. Hitler had a short conversation with him, then spoke to Ribbentrop on the telephone, and all this gave me time to pull myself together and to continue calmly when the dictation began again.

I've forgotten what the subject of that first text I typed for the Führer was: probably just an aide-memoire that wasn't going to be sent out. When I'd finished, I handed him the piece of paper. I'd been warned that I should leave wide spaces between the lines, in case he wanted to write in any corrections. He glanced over the sheet, assured me that it seemed perfectly all right, sat down at his desk and said goodbye.

In the antechamber I came face to face with Gruppenführer Bormann, who had been sitting there waiting for the dictation to finish, to find out whether it had gone well. When I told him that I thought I'd passed my 'exam', he seemed even more pleased than I was. Later I discovered that the relationship between him and his powerful brother Martin was far from cordial, and their rivalry even extended to insignificant things like employing a secretary. Fräulein Böttcher told me that Martin Bormann had wanted to present his own candidates to Hitler, so that the Führer's secretary would be in his confidence.

We were still talking when the door opened. Hitler appeared and came over and sat down beside us. He asked me several questions about my family and my previous jobs, then confirmed that my work had been very good. I thought to myself that he had nothing to compare it to, since he hadn't checked the other candidates' work, but he seemed to think this one test was enough and to have no desire to see the others.

A small voice inside my head told me that my fate was sealed, for better or for worse. I knew my mother wouldn't be at all pleased about the idea. She disliked Hitler. She thought he was responsible for the break-up of her marriage. After the First World War, when inflation and unemployment were at their worst, my father, like so many discharged soldiers, was without a job. So he joined a paramilitary movement called the Bund Oberland, far away in Silesia. This organisation gave a good many veterans a chance to survive, at least. But in the end Hitler and the new Nazi party claimed all my father's attention. My mother was bitterly unhappy at his departure, and took it as a rejection of the family. She took my sister and me and moved back to her parents' home.

The day after my dictation test with the Führer the other girls took a train back to Berlin, while I stayed at the Wolfsschanze. I moved out of the special train into the bunker where the other secretaries lived. I was issued with a pass, and found myself within a few hundred yards of the Führer's bunker. I wasn't at all happy about my new quarters, because I love light and fresh air and to me nothing could be worse than the atmosphere of a bunker. I had a sitting room which had some little windows, but at night I had to shut myself up in a cell not much bigger than my compartment on the special train but without any opening to the outside. A ventilator in the ceiling provided a form of air conditioning: if you shut it off, you suffocated, but when it was going it made an infernal racket. You felt as if you were on a plane. The other two secretaries, Fräulein Wolf and Fräulein Schroeder, preferred to sleep on the couch in their sitting room, which was at the front of the bunker and had a couple of big windows, so they'd turned it into a bedsit. I soon decided to follow their example, and so I fixed up my one room as best I could.

A long time afterwards, I found out why Hitler had made up his mind so quickly about choosing me. Like most Austrians and southern Germans, who are Catholics, he had no time for the Prussians. All the other candidates were Prussians. His Austrian accent was quite different from the Prussian way of speaking, and he felt much more at ease with a Bavarian from Munich like me. Munich was so dear to his heart, in fact, that it had been declared the 'Capital of the Nazi Movement'. He found it reassuring that my father had been a veteran of the 'days of combat' and, last but not least, that I'd been introduced to the Chancellery by Martin Bormann's brother.

5

Traudl Humps Becomes Hitler's Secretary

On 30 January 1943 – the tenth anniversary of the *Machtergreifung*, the seizure of power by the Nazis – I was called in to see Hitler. I felt just as nervous as the first time, because I didn't know whether it was another trial or whether my position was confirmed, even though I'd been at the Wolfsschanze for four weeks. I saw when I went in that the other two secretaries were there. I wondered whether I'd be expected to take an oath of allegiance, or go through some other formality. I felt uneasy. But Hitler turned to me and told me he was quite happy with my work, and that my two more experienced colleagues thought I had the right qualities to be his secretary. He asked if I wanted to stay in the job. I was twenty-two, I was completely ignorant about politics; I simply found it extraordinary that anyone should offer me a job like that. I said 'Yes' straightaway.

Hitler seemed to want to say something else, and appeared to be struggling for the right words. Eventually he gave an embarrassed grin and said, 'You're very young. There are a lot of men here, and most of them are away from home for a year at a time. . . .' I was to be very careful, he said, and to keep myself to myself; above all I was to come straight to him if I had any complaints about anyone. Instead of testing the strength of my National Socialist feelings, making me swear loyalty or giving me a lecture about confidentiality, Hitler was worrying about my virtue. It was a great relief, because I felt quite confident on that score and was able to reassure him, and to express my gratitude for his concern.

That was how I became one of Hitler's secretaries. From that day onwards, apart from a few holidays, it was rare for a day to go by without my working with him or sitting down to a meal with him.

Later that day I was sent for to take my first proper dictation from the Führer. It was an odd moment, right in the middle of a meal, but I left my lunch and made straight for the Führer's bunker. There, Hans Junge told me that Hitler wanted to dictate a speech to mark the tenth anniversary of the Nazis' coming to power. Although it had become a tradition for him to make a speech that day, this time the Führer wasn't going to appear in person but would broadcast over the radio, and his speech would also appear in the press.

I was shown into his inner office, which I hadn't had a chance to see before. To get there, one had to cross a narrow room with a low ceiling, lit only by electricity, then go through some large double doors in the vast area that surrounded Hitler's suite of offices. I greeted the Führer as soon as the valet announced me. As usual, he was wearing black trousers, a field-grey tunic with crossed-over fastenings, an immaculately white shirt and a black tie. I'd never seen him dressed any other way. The tunic was absolutely plain, with silver buttons, and on the left breast were pinned the golden insignia of the party and a First World War Iron Cross.

While he was busy giving instructions to the valet, I took the opportunity to look around in the full daylight cast by the windows. Almost the whole of one wall was taken up by a large table on which stood telephones, lamps and pencils. This was where the General Staff spread out their maps when they had briefing sessions on the situation at the various fronts. Several stools served as seats. Opposite the door, at the far end of the room, was Hitler's desk, an ordinary wooden desk such as could be found in any office at that time.

It was one o'clock, I noticed. I later discovered that Hitler always preferred to ask the time of whoever was there – despite the fact that he kept in his trouser pocket a large gold half-hunter watch.

Opposite the windows was a large fireplace, in front of which stood a circular table surrounded by eight armchairs with wicker seats and backs. There was a piece of furniture with a record player set into it, and several oak cupboards against the wall.

While I was inspecting the surroundings, I'd had time to get the typewriter ready and set out the paper. Hitler came over to me and asked, 'Are you sure you're not too cold, my dear? It's icy in here.' I automatically answered that I was quite all right, but I very soon regretted it, because while the dictation was in progress I realised that it was in fact freezing cold in the office.

Hitler started on his speech, walking backwards and forwards across the width of the room, his hands clasped behind his back, his head slightly lowered. I had to concentrate hard to catch what he said, because he spoke the words straight off, without referring to any notes, in the rhythm he would have used if he'd been addressing an audience. Luckily, there was nothing new he could say about the coming to power of the Nazis, and I knew most of the events by heart. Only at the end, when he began talking about the bitter fighting which would end in ultimate victory, did he raise his voice enough so that I no longer had to struggle to hear him, even when he was speaking behind my back from the far side of the room.

The dictation lasted an hour. I showed him the sheets of paper and told him that I might not have caught it all, but he gave a friendly smile and shook my hand, saying 'Don't worry. I'm sure it's all perfectly all right.'

When I left, my feet were frozen and my head was burning. I asked the valet outside why it was so cold in the office – couldn't the head of state allow himself a bit more heating? There was a central heating system that warmed all the rooms. 'The Führer likes to work in a very low temperature,' the valet replied, 'and won't have the room any warmer.' I realised why the generals always came out of their briefings, which sometimes lasted several hours, with red noses and blue hands. It was quite usual for them to rush straight to the mess or the valets' room to warm them-selves up with a glass of schnapps. General Jodl even claimed to have contracted chronic rheumatism as a result of conferences with Hitler.

I got used to this strange new world quite quickly. The forest and the landscape around us seemed to make the adjustment easier. We didn't really have any rules of work – there were no fixed hours, and no office atmosphere. I took long walks and revelled in the fresh air of the forests, and never for a moment regretted that I wasn't in the big city.

Hitler liked to make out that he'd chosen for his HQ the most swampy, mosquito-infested and least pleasant of places, but I thought it was magnificent. In winter, that part of East Prussia has an attraction that's hard to describe. I'll never forget the snow-covered birch trees, the limpid sky, the vast plains and the lakes. In summer, I had to admit the Führer was right, for millions of mosquitoes shared our quarters and fed on our blood, and the stuffy, humid air left us breathless.

When the weather was like this it was hard to convince Hitler to take his daily walk. He went to ground in the cool of his bunker and it was only out of love for his dog, Blondi, that he could be persuaded to go for a short walk after breakfast on the piece of land allocated for the purpose next to his bunker. That was where Blondi used to show off the tricks her master had taught her. She had become the most agile and best-trained animal one could imagine, and Hitler was always delighted if she managed to improve on her own high-jump record by several inches, or to stand balanced on a narrow bar for two or three extra minutes. He used to say that she was his best form of relaxation. She was surprising, certainly. She could wriggle through rubber tyres, jump up onto a six-feet-high wooden gate without any difficulty, climb to the top of a ladder and perform little tricks on the platform. It was a pleasure to see master and dog going through these exercises together, and a small group of spectators often used to gather on the edge of the area reserved for the Führer's walk to watch the games.

For the first few weeks, all I had to do was to find out every morning whether there was any work for me and to let the switchboard, or the valet on duty, know where I could be reached, so I had plenty of free time to observe Hitler's entourage.

Among the people closest to the Führer on a daily basis were the valets, Heinz Linge and Hans Junge, who swopped shifts every two days. They both belonged to the Leibstandarte SS, the SS bodyguard division, and they fulfilled functions that were as responsible as they were varied. Although they were called valets, that term doesn't give a clear picture of their duties. They were more like managers of Hitler's household, or perhaps Hitler's court; they accompanied him wherever he went and were his right-hand men. The valet on duty had to wake the Führer in the morning by knocking at his door, tell him the exact time and deliver the overnight news bulletin. It was his job to decide the day's menu, fix the mealtimes, give orders to the kitchen and serve Hitler's meals. Under the valet's orders was a staff officer who looked after the Führer's wardrobe and the upkeep of his apartments. It was the valets who called the barber or the dentist and who made sure the dogs were fed.

Nobody knew the Führer's peculiarities and habits – or his mood of the moment – better than Heinz Linge, a most tactful and devoted man. He was calm enough never to lose his self-control, and had a sense of humour which enabled him to dominate tricky situations. The most eminent personages and Hitler's closest colleagues never failed to check with Linge whether it was an opportune moment to take Hitler some bad news, and quite often Linge would suggest, with all due respect, that it would be better to wait until after the afternoon siesta, when Hitler was usually in a better mood. We secretaries were supposed to keep in constant contact with the valets, as it was they who let us know when we were needed.

Apart from the valets, the only permanent inhabitant of the bunker was Hitler's chief aide-de-camp, Gruppenführer Julius Schaub, whose SS rank was equivalent to that of colonel. From the historical point of view there's little reason to discuss this man at length, but at some time or other every one of us wondered how the head of state could tolerate the constant presence of someone so grotesque, and why he'd entrusted him with a job like that. I never really understood it.

Julius Schaub thought he was a very important person, and he never realised he was the only one of that opinion. When I scarcely knew him someone told me a revealing story about him. He'd been a member of the party since its beginnings, and so his party membership card had a very low number. One day someone asked him who formulated the policies of the National Socialist party; Schaub, who at the time had been nothing more than a manservant to Hitler, responsible for cleaning his shoes and so on, replied in his thick Bavarian accent: 'Myself and Hitler.'

Later on, when I knew him as chief aide-de-camp, so deaf that he perpetually held his hand cupped round his ear, and limping along on his little deformed feet, I always had difficulty repressing a smile. Nobody took him seriously, and yet he remained in his post and his orders had to be respected – unless he could be persuaded to change his mind by means of a glass of schnapps, which usually did the trick. Schaub had been wounded in the feet during the First World War. Later, when he joined the party, Hitler couldn't help noticing him: he was always there, hobbling along on his crutches, everywhere that Hitler went. One day, Hitler learned that this insignificant little man had lost his job because of his party membership, and he offered him a job as his manservant. Through a combination of usefulness and blind devotion Schaub very soon made himself indispensable to the Führer, and patiently hoisted himself into the job of aide-de-camp, then chief aide-de-camp. He was the only one of Hitler's entourage who had belonged to the old guard and taken part in the 'time of combat'; he was also the guardian of a large number of Hitler's secrets, which was perhaps another reason why the Führer chose not to get rid of him.

A barrack room at the HQ had been set up as a cinema, because when such a large number of soldiers are isolated in the middle of a forest it's as well to provide some distractions for the sake of morale. Every evening at eight o'clock a film was shown, and the programmes proved so popular that the cinema soon had to be enlarged. The only person who never went was Hitler. He used to have the newsreel of the week shown to him, so that he could censor any passages he wanted, but he never appeared when a film was projected, even if it was the première of a new German movie.

At these film showings I got friendly with many people who were part of the Führer's immediate circle but whom I had nothing to do with professionally. Among them were Professor Morell and Professor Karl Brandt. The first was Hitler's personal physician; the other a surgeon who travelled everywhere with the Führer and who later became Reich Commissioner for Health. The press officers often turned up for the films, too. The director of the Press Office, Otto Dietrich, who was always in uniform, looked like a little rodent and gave the impression of being an inoffensive, colourless person, whereas his colleague Heinz Lorenz, who usually wore civilian clothes, was a born journalist, full of good humour, charm and wit.

The generals rarely put in an appearance, because the briefing sessions on the situation at the front took place at the same time as the films. From time to time, though, they did attend, and we'd hear the gross guffaws of Martin Bormann, a person who was seldom seen around the HQ, although his signature appeared on all the order sheets and regulations which determined the management of the camp. A thickset, bull-necked man, he was one of the best-known and most feared characters at the Wolfsschanze, since he was responsible for the execution of all the orders given by the Führer. One of the nicest people I met, on the other hand, was Ambassador Walter Hewel. I'd noticed him at one of the first film shows I went to, because he laughed in such a good-hearted way that he carried the rest of the audience along with him.

One evening they showed us a German film called *A Mother's Love*, which was so naïvely sentimental that it made us all roar with laughter rather than cry, and I was very surprised at the end of the film to see two elderly men with their eyes brimming with tears. Nothing in their massive physiques made me expect such soft-heartedness. I asked Heinz Linge, who was sitting next to me, if he knew these officers, and I was amazed by the reply: the first was SS Oberführer Rattenhuber, head of the Secret Service, and the other was the Commissioner for Criminal Affairs, Höge. It was the job of these men to look after the Führer's security in the camp.

After these film shows I was never short of company in the mess, but we never talked about politics. If the serious problems of the war were ever mentioned it was always in the context of the certainty of ultimate victory and absolute confidence in the Führer. Behind this optimistic façade, each of us hid his or her personal feelings. There was never any question of voicing it aloud, but after the defeat at Stalingrad doubt had already begun to grow in many people's minds.

As for me at the age of twenty-two, a newcomer in this male community, I let myself be convinced by this overt optimism. Later I often wondered how I could have felt at ease among those people, but I think that the barriers and barbed wire fences that surrounded us made many of our doubts disappear. We had no access to information apart from the communiqués from the front, especially not to the foreign radio broadcasts that many other Germans listened to. I didn't read the newspapers and anyway, having grown up during the spread of the Nazi movement, I had absolutely no knowledge of the outside world and no point of comparison. Besides, it had been severely impressed upon me by Julius Schaub that I mustn't divulge the tiniest detail of my work to anyone, and of course the same orders applied to everyone who worked in the camp. To express a doubt would have been tantamount to treason.

6

Dinner with Hitler En Route to Bavaria

Almost two months had passed since my arrival at the Wolfsschanze. I had got used to life at the camp and made friends with some of the residents. The days passed calmly and without incident until one morning when, as soon as I woke up, I became aware of an unusual amount of coming and going. Orderlies were rushing back and forth between the Führer's bunker and Julius Schaub's. Vehicles were accelerating away. An orderly arrived to summon me to see Schaub, who greeted me in a solemn and mysterious manner. He handed me a piece of paper – a travel plan. He told me that the Führer was to fly to the Eastern Front, and that this document was top secret. He really wanted me to type it out without reading it, obviously. I hurried away to type the text, which turned out to contain nothing but instructions to drivers and pilots and the list of people who were going on the journey. But I did discover that Hitler was going to Vinnitsa, on the Eastern Front, to visit the army HQ. The other passengers were to be one of the valets, two orderlies, a doctor, the aides-de-camp and a few others. I wasn't on the list.

By one o'clock that day the bunker was deserted, and an extraordinary calm reigned over the camp as if the engine of a huge machine had suddenly stopped. It was then that I felt for the first time the extent to which Hitler's remarkable personality supplied the driving force for all those people. He was the puppet master who held in his hands the strings controlling the whole theatre of marionettes, and he had suddenly let them fall.

Much later, after the war, I discovered that the Führer had only returned safe and sound from this inspection of the Russian Front

43

by chance, because the first of several plots against his life accidentally failed. As soon as his visit was known, a group of high-ranking officers with General von Tresckow at their head had put into action their plan to eliminate him. An explosive device which had been carefully tested in advance was put inside a cognac bottle and wrapped up as a gift for Colonel Stieff, a member of the General Staff of the War Ministry in Berlin. Just as Hitler's plane was leaving, the package was handed to one of the group aboard the plane, who was supposed to pass it on to Colonel Stieff. But for unknown reasons the mechanism failed to work, and the plane landed safely. The members of the conspiracy, who reappeared at the time of the assassination attempt of 20 July 1944, were luckily able to contact the person to whom the 'gift' was addressed, pretend that there had been a mistake and recover the parcel – so no one in Hitler's entourage knew about the failed plot. The next day Lieutenant Fabian von Schlabrendorff managed to get aboard a mail plane, find the officer who had been handed the package, and replace it with another containing a bottle of Cointreau. If the bomb had exploded it would have killed the Führer and everyone on his plane; as it was, Hitler never even knew that in March 1943 his life hung by a thread.

Our daily routine at the Wolfsschanze returned to normal after Hitler's trip, but not for long. A few days later I was asked to type out another set of travel plans, and this time my name and those of the other secretaries were on the list. The entire General Staff was to move to Berchtesgaden in Bavaria, or more precisely, to the Berghof mountain retreat in Obersalzburg. The Führer needed rest, and would take the opportunity to receive some state visits. In actual fact it had been decided that the Wolfsschanze HQ wasn't sufficiently secure, and they were to start work on extra fortifications. So at the end of March 1943 I was able to take part in the dismantling and transfer of a gigantic military installation.

The move was planned several weeks in advance, but the way in which the preparations went ahead – swiftly and without the slightest hitch – was impressive to watch. We three secretaries were responsible for ensuring that a travelling office functioned smoothly for the duration of the journey, because the Führer might need to draft an order or a report for his generals at any moment. We took with us two ordinary typewriters, two typewriters with capital letters and one special machine with extra-large letters so that the Führer could read his speeches

Traudl Humps, aged 23, goes swimming near the Wolfsschanze.

With the Goebbels and three of their children — Helga, Helmut and Hilde. All five Goebbels children had names beginning with the letter 'H' in honour of Hitler.

Above: Hans Baur.

Right: Otto Günsche.

The Berghof, Hitler's mountain retreat.

The dining room at the Berghof.

The sitting room
at the Berghof.

A corner of Eva
Braun's bedroom
at the Berghof.
The door on the
right led into
Hitler's bedroom.
(*Paris Match*).

Above and below: Hitler and Eva were both fond of dogs. Hers were called Stasi and Negus and his was called Blondi. *(Below: Popperfoto).*

Gerda Christian ('Dara') and Christa Schroeder congratulating Hitler on his birthday. (*Paris Match*).

In the tea-house. The other guests would continue their conversation when Hitler dropped off to sleep. (*Paris Match*).

Above: Eva wore elegant couture clothes from top German and Italian designers. *(Paris Match).*

Left: Hitler and Eva with the daughter of Eva's friend Herta Schneider. The child was often photographed with them and some people have mistakenly claimed that she was their child. *(Popperfoto).*

without spectacles. A trunk with several compartments and drawers contained letterhead of different types and all the necessary office equipment. Hitler used a variety of headed paper for his letters. In his capacity as head of state the heading was the national emblem, the eagle and swastika, and beneath that 'The Führer' engraved in gold. For letters of a more personal sort, he used similar large white sheets without the emblem but with the inscription 'Adolf Hitler' engraved in the same gold script. There was a third kind of paper for letters concerning the party or military affairs, on which the eagle and swastika were printed in black.

For the details of the move itself Hitler gave orders and instructions to Bormann or to Field Marshal Keitel, who transmitted them to the individuals or services concerned. Each one had to ensure that they could continue their work during the journey.

The lion's share of the work was done by the two aides-de-camp, Fritz Darges and Otto Günsche. They organised everything, arranging the transportation of materials, checking the timetable of the special train which was always standing by wherever Hitler was, and giving instructions to the personnel who were to remain in the camp. Everything was accomplished in the greatest secrecy and as quickly as possible.

The departure was fixed for 21.30 hours. Everyone had received the number of their carriage and their seat. As soon as the car containing Hitler, his valet, an aide-de-camp and Blondi arrived, the Führer climbed into his carriage and the train set off into the clear, soft winter's night. As we moved away in total darkness, I stared through the window of my compartment at the snow-covered forest landscape. My heart lurched and I was overcome by a feeling of apprehension about what was ahead.

I went out into the corridor. The train was so smooth and quiet that we hardly realised we were moving at all. It struck me that, even if the entire GHQ was changing its location, we were taking the atmosphere I was used to with us. My compartment was more luxurious than any of the rooms at the Wolfsschanze. During the day, the bed could be turned into a modern couch upholstered in shot silk with a pattern of multicoloured flowers on a pale beige background. The walls were of varnished wood. In the toilets there was hot and cold running water, and on a little table by the window stood a bronze lamp. A wall telephone above the bed meant easy contact with other compartments; the floor was covered with a velvety carpet.

The two carriages containing the guest quarters were next to the restaurant car, which was used as a mess. Following that came the carriages where the Führer's service personnel were lodged, as well as the teletype operators, the guards and the orderlies. Then came a carriage furnished as a conference room, where the briefing sessions on the situation at the front were held around a large table made out of exotic wood. The seats were covered in red leather, and various lamps and other forms of lighting could be plugged in all around the room. Before the war the carriage was used for receptions, and was shown to foreign visitors as a curiosity. There were also a record player and a radio in the carriage, but I never knew them to be used. The adjoining carriage contained Hitler's personal apartments and his private bathroom. Elsewhere on the train a whole carriage was filled with shower cubicles and hip baths, and there were a few carriages for the train staff and the soldiers who manned the anti-aircraft defences to protect us against a low-altitude attack.

There we were, rolling through the night across the whole length of Germany, from north to south, in exceptionally comfortable conditions, and I thought of all the other trains criss-crossing Germany in the cold and dark at that moment, full of soldiers and ordinary people who were probably hungry and didn't even have room to sit down. I felt suddenly guilty: it was easy to support a war when one didn't feel the consequences personally. For me it was quite the opposite, in fact – I would never have had the chance to live in such luxurious conditions in peacetime.

I was shaken out of these thoughts by an orderly who'd come to tell me that Hitler had invited me to dinner. I rushed into the next-door compartment to ask my colleague Johanna Wolf whether she'd been invited as well. She told me that she had, and that when the Führer was travelling he liked to take his meals with a few colleagues and his secretaries. Caught off guard, I told Fräulein Wolf that I hadn't got anything to wear except ordinary suits and jerseys, but she assured me that these dinners were quite informal. I went back to my compartment, powdered my nose and put on a touch of lipstick, then made my way with the other two secretaries to the Führer's carriage.

The table was set for eight people, but the Führer hadn't yet arrived. I wondered what we'd get to eat: I knew he was a vegetarian, but I didn't know whether his guests were allowed meat. The first of the other guests to arrive was Dr Morell, who had some difficulty in making his way through the narrow space behind the chairs – a space designed for people of normal girth. Hitler's doctor had never seemed so fat before. Ambassador Hewel, who came in next, wasn't particularly thin either, but he was tall and well-proportioned. He was, as usual, so relaxed that he helped me conquer my shyness. He switched on a lamp on the table, so that we could see what we were eating, he said, then declared that if Hitler was very late he'd go and fetch the sandwiches he'd brought with him, because he was very hungry. Just then the Führer appeared, followed by Schaub and Bormann. He shook us all by the hand and asked us to sit down, then took his place at the head of the table with Fräulein Wolf on his right and Fräulein Schroeder on his left. I was seated between Hewel and Bormann, and at the other end of the table Dr Morell squeezed himself in with great difficulty opposite Schaub.

It was all quite simple and relaxed. Heinz Linge served Hitler with potato purée and a fried egg, accompanied by a glass of sparkling Fachinger water and some wholemeal bread. I've forgotten what the rest of us ate: I was so busy taking everything in that I didn't eat much anyway. The conversation around the table was light and general, but I didn't take part unless someone asked me a question. Bormann was making a great effort to be sociable. He didn't seem at all like the powerful and frightening man I'd heard about.

Hitler was a congenial host and very attentive towards the women, encouraging us to help ourselves and asking whether there was anything else we wanted. He spoke quite wittily about other similar journeys he'd made, and joked with some of the guests, usually chatting in a quiet voice. He asked for the ceiling lights to be turned out; he preferred low lighting because his eyes were sensitive. A single lamp lit the compartment, the train rocked us with its regular movement and Professor Morell gradually began to doze off, which nobody seemed to mind. It was late. We were served with coffee and little cakes, while Hitler drank an infusion of cumin which he spoke very highly of. He tried to make Fräulein Schroeder taste it, but she wouldn't be convinced. The party didn't break up for some time. I must have eaten countless meals with the Führer but that first dinner aboard the train sticks in my memory as an unexpected event. I paid very little attention to what Hitler actually talked about during the meal, as I was most absorbed by the way in which he talked and what this revealed about his personality.

From time to time the train stopped at a station, and immediately the liaison officers would set up telephone lines for urgent communications. The aides-de-camp ran back and forth with messages. The Führer never forgot about Blondi, and always asked Linge to take her out onto the platform.

Hitler addressed his colleagues by their surnames. He'd say: 'Linge, take Blondi for a walk', or 'Bormann, what time is it?' On this occasion, as we sat round the table in Hitler's saloon carriage late at night, Bormann's answer was 'Half past one'. Hitler called Linge again to ask him whether there had been any reports of enemy flights during the night – the reply was negative – and after that Hitler shook us all by the hand and went to bed.

Suddenly, I didn't feel tired any more. The coffee had woken me up. We went back to our compartments after a brief halt in the restaurant car to smoke a cigarette, and eventually I too went to bed.

I was woken up by the sound of footsteps in the corridor. It was nine o'clock and we were scheduled to arrive in Munich at midday. Outside, the sun was shining and the trees were thickly covered with a fresh layer of snow. I hurriedly got dressed and went to have breakfast. At the table everyone was talking about the Berghof and Eva Braun, whom I was dying to meet. She was supposed to be joining the train in Munich and continuing the journey as far as Berchtesgaden, and I was curious to see what she'd be like with Hitler. Lieutenant Junge, whom I got on very well with and loved chatting to, had told me that Eva Braun was mistress of the house at the Berghof, and recognised as such by everyone who stayed there. Junge said I should get used to the idea that the Berghof was the Führer's private domain; we were his guests, and we'd have all our meals with him. This was certainly true for the inner circle – his immediate colleagues and a few intimate friends – but the rest of the General Staff, and his chief acolytes such as Goering, Bormann and Goebbels, were housed in separate buildings around the Berghof, while the officers and men of the Chancellery and the military command had quarters in Berchtesgaden.

The town of Berchtesgaden is situated at the foot of the Bavarian Alps in a region known as the Salzkammergut because of the saltmines in the area. A steep mountain road leads out of the town up to where the Berghof, a spacious stone villa, used to stand. When the American forces arrived they dynamited the Berghof. It was Hitler's principal residence when he wasn't in

Berlin or at one of the GHQs close to the front. During the war a bunker for protection against air raids had been built beside the Berghof itself.

Nearby was the Eagle's Nest, of which Hitler was particularly fond. Perched at a height of just over 6000 feet, the terrace had a view which extended right into Austria; in clear weather it was a breathtaking panorama which impressed all the Führer's guests, including the many visiting heads of state he entertained there. In the vast tea room with wide bay windows one had the impression of being suspended over a void. To reach the Eagle's Nest there was a tunnel carved out of the rock, and the whole gigantic enterprise had been built by the workers of the Todt Organisation to celebrate the Führer's fiftieth birthday in 1939.

The Eagle's Nest still exists intact; however, it is closed to visitors and one can only admire the view of the valley from the platform surrounding the building. After the war, when a resurgence of Nazism was still feared, it was considered possible that all these buildings might become places of neo-Nazi pilgrimage under the pretext of tourism.

Before going up to the Berghof we were to spend a day in Munich, and I was tremendously excited about the prospect of seeing my family. I'd been away from them for six months. At long last the train drew up in the station on the platform beside the train carrying the rest of the GHQ personnel, which had arrived some time earlier. When we left our carriages and made our way towards the special exit, there was no sign of the Führer. He had been the first to leave the train, and his car had been waiting to drive him to his private house at No. 16 Prinzregenten-platz. This modest, three-storey house which the party had bought for him still exists. After the war it became a police station. It was in that house that Geli Raubal, Hitler's niece, had killed herself with his pistol while he was out at a propaganda meeting.

Hitler had brought Geli (short for Angelika) and her mother from Berchtesgaden to live in Munich; while her mother acted as the housekeeper, Geli had become Hitler's mistress, and there seems no doubt that she was one of the two great passions of his life. He seems to have been deeply in love with Geli, whereas in his long liaison with Eva Braun sensuality at first played the most important part, though later he came to admire her other qualities such as devotion and courage.

I hurried to get to my mother's house as fast as I could. I was longing to see her, and anxious to tell her all that had happened to me at first hand. She hadn't approved of my decision and the paraphernalia surrounding my new position as the Führer's secretary didn't impress her at all. She would have preferred me to keep my more modest job in Munich. Her maternal instinct foresaw the dangers I was running, morally and physically. But I'd gone into the whirlpool of life in the Führer's entourage without a single backward glance, happy to escape the mediocre existence of an ordinary office worker and hungry for new experience.

7

At the Berghof

That evening, the snow began to fall again. The train left
discreetly, shortly after dusk. I didn't see Hitler again until we
arrived at Liefering, a small town near Salzburg, and then all I
saw were the back lights of his big Mercedes disappearing in the
direction of Obersalzberg, followed by a long line of vehicles. I'd
taken my place beside my colleagues in one of the cars, and we
were driving towards the mountains. Before long the procession
of cars began to climb a steep, winding road up to a height of
3000 feet. The Berghof was in sight. The great building stood
out in the night sky and the wide bay windows of the hall reflected
the whiteness of the snow that covered everything thickly. Two
lamps shone above the front door, lighting the steps up to it.

Hitler had arrived shortly before us and had immediately disappeared into his own rooms. His coat and hat were hanging in the
hall. We were greeted by Frau Mittelstrasser, the housekeeper, a
small woman from Munich with a polite but energetic manner,
who was apparently very efficient. She guided the new arrivals
towards a large hall and the staircase leading to our rooms. My
room and Fräulein Schroeder's were high up under the roof, in
an old part of the house which used to be called Haus Wachenfeld.
It had belonged to Hitler's half-sister Angela, Geli's mother, but
since its incorporation into the Berghof it had all been changed,
renovated and modernised. My bedroom was charming – very
feminine, with a desk, a large bed and upholstery in sky blue and
white. Fräulein Schroeder's was much the same but with a colour
scheme in red.

Although I came from Munich, I'd never had the chance to see
the mountains so close to. The first day, as soon as I opened the
shutters I expected to be able to admire the scenery everyone

talked about so enthusiastically, but I was in for a disappointment. All I saw was a thick wall of impenetrable fog, with no trace of a mountain in sight: what's more, I came to realise that these were the region's most common weather conditions.

That first morning I wanted to get to know the inside of the Berghof as quickly as I could, and I also wanted some breakfast. I went back down the staircase we'd climbed the previous evening. From the staircase I went into an antechamber on the ground floor, where another glass door led into a rustic-style room with a huge green porcelain stove, but still nothing suggested breakfast. I pushed open another set of double doors that looked as if they might lead into the great hall that was so well known at the time because of the countless postcards and reproductions featuring it. Behind that, I discovered a wide passage with walls covered in marble and found myself at long last in a big dining room where a whole group of people were already eating breakfast.

It was a long room which took up most of one wing of the new part of the building. In the middle was a huge round table surrounded by armchairs, which seated twenty-four people. The room's only decoration was the beautiful natural pine panelling; the furniture and even the light fittings above the table were made of the same material, and a few precious vases added a touch of colour to the overall beige and gold colour scheme.

My colleague Christa Schroeder seemed a bit put out that I was late, but nobody had thought to tell me about the timetable of the household. The group around the table included General Schmundt, then Chief of General Staff of the Wehrmacht, Captain von Puttkammer, naval aide-de-camp, and Walter Frentz, a photographer attached to the GHQ. The breakfast menu was varied, with a choice of tea, coffee, cocoa or fruit juice and a whole range of different sorts of bread and biscuits, including rye bread and ordinary black bread; white bread was only for those with delicate stomachs, though. Everyone had a ration of ten grammes of butter, which was already on our plates, and there was jam as well.

Since no one was allowed to smoke in any of the rooms the Führer used, the guests dispersed straight after breakfast to light their cigarettes. Otto Günsche, Christa Schroeder and I set off on a tour of inspection of our new abode. Since I was keen to see where the Führer himself lived, we began by going up the main staircase. It came out into a very wide corridor, almost a hall in its own right, with large windows, walls hung with valuable classical paintings, fine statues and exotic vases – all presents from foreign heads of state. The impression was of being in a museum. Everything was beautiful, but completely cold and impersonal.

It was as quiet as the grave, because Hitler was still asleep. At the top of the staircase, the first door on the left led into a little apartment of two rooms and a bathroom used by the valet on duty and the chauffeur. Opposite was a linen room for Eva Braun's maids. In front of one door lay two Scotch terriers, Stasi and Negus, the bodyguards of the lady of the house, who waited patiently until she woke up and allowed them to greet her noisily. The neighbouring door was the Führer's bedroom. Between the two rooms was a large bathroom which had no door out onto the passage. A large set of double doors opened into Hitler's office, where I hadn't yet been, and opposite Eva Braun's bedroom were two or three steps which led down into the passage that connected the old house – Haus Wachenfeld, where Fräulein Schroeder and I had our attic rooms – and the main Berghof building.

In the living room, which I'd quickly glanced into earlier that morning, there was nobody to be found except two or three orderlies busy finishing their work. I gathered that this used to be Hitler's sitting room. It was furnished in the traditional way, and was just like a comfortable room in the house of any well-to-do middle-class family; none the less, it was the only room with any feeling of warmth about it. A large green porcelain stove was surrounded by a bench which seemed to invite you to relax. In front of the big window stood a square table, and in the corner was a wooden seat. The tablecloth, the curtains and the upholstery of the bench were all made out of the same brightly coloured peasant fabric. On the wall opposite the window was a large bookcase which contained numerous volumes of a big dictionary, a few major works of international literature with little sign of having been opened very often, Wilhelm Busch's works, a series of travel books, and, of course, *Mein Kampf* bound in leather. Anyone was allowed to borrow any of these books.

A high curtain separated this living room from the great hall. As soon as I glanced inside it, I had the same impression I'd had from the postcards: it was too big, too rich, as impressive as everything the Führer had built but far too cold despite the thick carpets, the fine Gobelins tapestries and all the valuable ornaments. Later on, when we used to sit there by candlelight around the fire, the same feeling never left me: that room was much too big and the people in it much too small to fill it.

On the other hand, the winter garden one passed through to get from the living room onto the terrace was very much to my taste. It was full of flowers, and furnished with little seats and stools covered with soft, pale-coloured fabric. The terrace itself was the most beautiful feature of the Berghof. It was a paved rectangular area with a stone parapet from which, whenever the thick mist lifted, one could see in the distance the citadel of Salzburg on its soft hillside bathed in sunlight. On the other side, Berchtesgaden stretched out below, bordered by mountains – Watzmann, Hoher Göll and the Steinernes Meer. The Unterberg rose up immediately opposite, and on a clear day one could see the cross on the summit with one's naked eye. The terrace ran all the way round the winter garden up to the windows of the sitting room, and ended in a paved courtyard which stretched round the other side of the building and was closed off by the rock face as if by a wall.

From the rear exit of the Berghof, or from the terrace, there was access to the office of the aides-de-camp. On the ground floor was a small office for the press and Ambassador Hewel; the next storey was reserved for the aide-de-camp on duty, Gruppenführer Bormann or Obergruppenführer Schaub, who had the use of a charming rustic apartment consisting of a sitting room, a bedroom and a bathroom which was reached by an exterior wooden staircase, very picturesque but dangerous in the rain or snow. This little house was extended by a wooden structure used for various things, but temporarily allocated as our office. It was very dark, with grubby, worn-out furniture, and I never understood why the place was left in such a miserable state – unless it was because Hitler had never set foot in it. There wasn't even enough light to see by, because a passage with a wooden roof ran the whole length of the building and blocked out all the light.

Next to our office was a dental surgery for Professor Blaschke and his assistant, who came from Berlin when someone needed them. Although it was small, his surgery had all the most up-to-date equipment, because Hitler was in the habit of having his teeth seen to while he was staying in the mountains. There was also a rudimentary hairdresser's salon in the same place. Next came a large dormitory for the soldiers on guard duty, and at the far end of that the limits of the garden and the gate leading to the

Berghof guest house. A sentry was always there, demanding to see an official pass whenever anyone came or went.

Immediately below the Berghof ran the road that zigzagged up from the valley to the heights of the Platterhof, Bormann's house and the barracks. On the far side of the road was a marvellous stretch of land that fell gently away towards the foot of the mountain. No landscape gardener could have designed it better. The fields, the forests and the streams formed a natural park, and the only signs of human interference were the well-tended paths and the road. Down there, camouflaged in the woods and invisible from the Berghof, was hidden what the staff called Hitler's 'escape': a little tea house where he went almost every day.

Despite my strong feelings for all this natural beauty, I never felt relaxed at the Berghof. We were treated as guests, it's true; but we weren't there voluntarily, we were only employees. The only people who enjoyed their stay were the men who could bring their families or install their wives in Berchtesgaden or the surrounding area, and even they suffered mixed feelings because although they knew their loved ones were nearby it was hard for them to come and go freely. Only the people who had a clearly defined function that was not associated with Hitler's daily routine could take full advantage of the Berghof's charms. Everyone else lived in the atmosphere of perpetual tension which characterised Hitler's day-to-day existence – an atmosphere which was exhausting, irregular, yet at the same time monotonous.

Throughout the morning, the whole building was so quiet that it seemed abandoned, apart from a semblance of life in the aides-de-camp's office. Things began to happen about midday. Cars driven at top speed deposited generals and officers for the daily briefing session. The terrace filled up with uniformed men who were desperate to smoke a cigarette and could only do it there; in the winter garden the ordnance officers waited with their files and their maps. It was only when the Führer appeared that everyone went back inside the house. Then the great hall with its enormous window, which seemed to have been designed for friendly contact and peaceful conversations, became the scene of animated argument and cold life-or-death decisions.

Meanwhile, more and more people would arrive, most of whom had nothing to do with the conference but who were hoping for an invitation to lunch. Otto Dietrich, the Chief Press Officer, and Heinz Lorenz, the Foreign Press Officer, usually came down from the guest house at the same time as Hitler's second personal physician, Dr von Hasselbach. Several days after our arrival various ladies appeared: Frau Brandt, wife of one of the doctors, Frau von Below, the wife of the Luftwaffe attaché, Frau Schneider, a close friend of Eva Braun's, and Gretl, Eva's sister. These last two were always among the regular guests at the Berghof.

Frau Brandt deserves a few words because Hitler felt great friendship for her. Born Annie Kehborn, she was an exceptionally good swimmer and at the age of nineteen had won the German Championship and a bronze medal at the European Championships of 1927. The Führer had been so impressed by her that in 1924, before he knew her, he had written her a letter of congratulations from the prison where he was sent after the failed putsch of 1923. In 1933 her fiancé had successfully operated on a party veteran and aide-de-camp of Hitler's, Wilhelm Brückner, who had been seriously hurt in a car accident while driving with Hitler in Berchtesgaden. Hitler was so impressed by the outcome that he declared that if ever he should need an operation it must be performed only by Brandt. The following year Brandt married Annie Kehborn; Hitler and Goering were witnesses at the wedding.

For as long as the briefing session at the Berghof lasted nobody went into the living room or the hall. We were supposed to wait in our rooms until we were called. Unfortunately Hitler seemed quite oblivious to hunger, and he often forgot that he had a roomful of lunch guests waiting for their meal and drinking vermouth after vermouth to keep their hunger pangs at bay. Sometimes it wasn't until three or four o'clock that the last uniform disappeared in the last official car and Hitler walked back up the few steps into the living room, where his famished guests had almost despaired of his arrival. At the very same moment Eva Braun would appear, heralded by the barking of her two black terriers. Hitler would kiss her hand, then greet each of the guests he hadn't seen during the conference.

At my first lunch there I saw Eva Braun for the first time and was introduced to her. I was struck by the ease and naturalness of her manner, though she wasn't at all like the ideal German girl who appeared on the posters of the BDM (Union of German Girls) or in the magazines of the time. Her coiffed hair was lightly bleached, and her pretty face wore very tasteful make-up. She wasn't tall but she had a good figure and carried herself well. She had a marvellous dress sense, was very carefully groomed, and knew her own style perfectly; she always wore valuable jewellery without ever looking over-dressed. When I saw her for the first time she was wearing a soft green dress in thick wool with a fitted top and a flared bell skirt with a broad leopardskin belt. The sleeves hugged the line of her arms and the heart-shaped neckline was held by two gold clips.

Eva was usually known by the title of *Gnädiges Fräulein*, but the wives of the senior figures called her Fräulein Braun. Frau Brandt and Frau von Below seemed great friends of hers. They chatted together in a natural and relaxed way about the usual feminine subjects: clothes, children, their dogs, their daily lives. Frau Schneider, whom Eva called by her first name, Herta, was an old schoolfriend and almost always with her, even in Munich. She was the mother of two little blonde girls who often appeared in photos with Eva Braun and whom people tended to mistake for children Eva might have had with Hitler.

While waiting for lunch to be served Hitler usually chatted to Eva, teasing her about her dogs, which he called the 'hearth brushes'. She'd reply by saying that Blondi wasn't so much a dog as a calf. I was astonished to see how this man, who'd just left a conference on the situation at the front, could free his mind so fast from all the increasingly serious problems he faced, just as if he had left them behind the heavy curtain separating the hall from the living room. His face was that of any good-humoured host entertaining friends in his country house.

Finally, the valet Linge came up to Frau Brandt and said, 'Madam, the Führer will escort you to lunch.' An orderly passed a seating plan around the other guests, then Linge turned to Hitler and said, 'Lunch is served, *mein Führer*.' Hitler, who had been told whose arm he was to take, went in first with Frau Brandt, followed by Eva Braun on the arm of Reichsleiter Martin Bormann – that order was never changed – with the other couples behind them. The Führer sat in the centre of the table, facing the windows, with Eva Braun on his left, and opposite them would sit the couple or individual of highest rank among that day's guests.

My neighbour at table that first day was the Chief Press Officer. He was in civilian clothes, a navy blue suit, which made him look less solemn than his uniform would. I was expecting a conversation about high political matters, but I was in for a disappointment. He asked me if it was my first time in the area and when I told him that I came from Munich but had never been in the mountains before he was as amazed as if I'd stepped down from the moon. He launched into an interminable list, complete with every last detail, of all the walks and trips I could take; the only benefit of this dull conversation was that it gave me a chance to watch the ceremony with which meals were conducted.

In the middle of the table there was a beautiful floral arrangement, which seemed surprising since there had never been a flower in sight in the dining room at the Wolfsschanze. Here, though, the hand of the lady of the house was in evidence. The table was laid with white Rosenthal china edged with a hand-painted flower pattern, and beside each place was a napkin in a little pochette with the guest's name on it.

No sooner had we sat down than the large door leading to the kitchen swung open and the orderlies came in. Two of them carried piles of heated plates to replace those already in front of us on the table. Hans Junge carried the Führer's special meal on a tray, and other orderlies handed round large bowls containing a variety of salads. Two more orderlies filled the glasses. The second course was roast meat with mashed potatoes and green beans. I'd already established with some relief, on the train journey, that Hitler's guests weren't expected to share his vegetarian diet. I often wondered what appalling illness would be serious enough to make me stick to a diet of oatmeal soup, mashed linseed, muesli and fruit juices.

At mealtimes Hitler often talked about how hard it was for a vegetarian to get more appetising dishes, but he complained of stomach pains which made it essential for him to follow a diet. As time went by I became convinced that most of his illnesses were nervous in origin or even partly imaginary. Here in Obersalzberg Hitler followed the regime of a Professor Zabel who had a sanatorium in Berchtesgaden, and who was a disciple of the nutritional theories of the Swiss Professor Bircher-Benner. Whenever Hitler stayed at the Berghof, a cook was sent up from the sanatorium to prepare his meals.

He had an extraordinary passion for raw linseed oil. For instance, he'd relish potatoes baked in the oven with this oil poured over them. Eva Braun regarded his eating habits with a mixture of pity and contempt, and nothing in the world would have persuaded her to taste his dishes. Nevertheless, she claimed to have a delicate stomach herself and ate very little – only light food containing hardly any fat. When I knew her better I realised that she was doing this mainly for the sake of her figure: she couldn't stand heavy women and was very proud of being so slim and elegant. Hitler used to tease her about it.

'When I first met you, you were nice and chubby, and now you're as thin as a rail. Women are always saying they want to be attractive to their men, but then they go and do the very opposite. They claim they'd sacrifice everything for him, but actually they just blindly follow the fashion. Fashion's the only important thing for them. What they care about most is what other women think: all they want is to make their friends jealous.'

Eva used to protest furiously, but she conceded that she wouldn't want to put on weight for anything in the world.

The conversation at mealtimes was always animated, but always superficial. Hitler would recount pranks he had played during his student days and lots of stories from the party's 'time of combat'. He often teased his colleagues. Walter Hewel, then a minister plenipotentiary and responsible for liaison with the Ministry of Foreign Affairs, was one of the Führer's favourite targets. Hewel was relatively young for his career rank – he was about forty – and he wasn't married. He spoke with a very exaggerated Rhineland accent and had lived in India for a long time. He could tell fascinating stories about that country.

Hitler asked him, 'When are you going to write your memoirs? You could call it *My Life as a Bushman and a Diplomat*. But you aren't really a diplomat, of course, just a big diplomatic cowboy.'

To which Hewel replied, 'If I weren't a diplomat, I wouldn't have lasted long liaising between you and Ribbentrop.' Hitler appreciated that answer, because he knew what a difficult man the Minister of Foreign Affairs was.

Hewel's bachelor life was another subject for daily jokes. 'You're waiting for a little Indian she-monkey to come along,' Hitler used to say to him. In fact Hitler was always trying to find a good match for his favourite diplomat. There was a time when most people in Hitler's entourage thought he wanted to see him married to Gretl Braun, Eva's sister; later on, his name was discreetly linked with that of Ilse Todt, daughter of the head of the Todt Organisation, the vast labour set-up that had built huge defences such as the Siegfried Line on the German–French border and the Atlantic Wall on the western coast of France. Hitler often used to say, in Hewel's hearing, what a beautiful girl Ilse was, and he was disappointed by Hewel's lack of reaction.

Hitler also enjoyed teasing the women at mealtimes. Noticing one day that Eva's table napkin had lipstick marks on it, he went into a long dissertation on the ingredients that, according to him, were used for making it. 'Do you know what a lipstick is made of?' he demanded.

Someone timidly offered a suggestion. 'Plant aphids, perhaps?' Frau Speer, wife of the Armaments Minister Albert Speer, thought she'd read that in a magazine.

Eva Braun said she only ever used French lipstick, and she was sure that it was made with only the purest ingredients.

Hitler gave her a pitying smile. 'If you knew that even in Paris lipstick is made from animal fats extracted from sewage, I'm sure that none of you would use it!'

We didn't take him seriously, because we knew that if he couldn't actually forbid something he tried to make us feel disgusted with it. All the women, apart from Martin Bormann's wife, went on wearing lipstick in front of the Führer.

Sometimes Hitler amused himself by spoiling the carnivores' pleasure in their food. He claimed he wasn't trying to convert anyone to vegetarianism, of course, but he took a delight in talking about his memories of a slaughterhouse he'd been invited to visit when the GHQ was stationed in the Ukraine. It was the largest and most modern in the whole area and was entirely mechanised, with a continuous process that turned live pigs into sausages, including the treatment of the bones, the offal and the other scraps. Everything about it was clean and well organised, down to the pretty young girls in rubber boots who worked standing in streams of blood up to their ankles. Some of the meat-eating officers who were with him were taken sick and had to slip away before the visit was over. 'That couldn't happen to me,' Hitler used to say. 'I can watch someone pulling up a beetroot, or collecting an egg, or dealing with a cow without any trouble.'

Most of the regular guests were used to this talk, and didn't lose their appetite because of it. But Hitler always managed to find one victim. On that first day it was the Chief Press Officer who turned pale, pushed his knife and fork to one side and timidly announced that he wasn't hungry. The Führer took the opportunity to deliver a general remark. 'That shows how cowardly people are,' he said. 'They can't face doing certain horrible things themselves, can't even bear to watch them being done, but they enjoy the benefits without a single pang of conscience.'

8

Tea House Conversation and Table Talk

Lunch usually lasted about an hour. Afterwards the Führer would get up and set off for a walk that had become a ritual. In fact he liked the walk itself less than its object: the tea house in the nearby fields. Even though it was quite close, about twenty minutes' walk away, he often tried to find an excuse to use the small Volkswagen. The valets and orderlies asked each of the guests if they wanted to go on the walk, but one was allowed to decline the offer and spend the afternoon as one wished. The few women were particularly welcome as company. Martin Bormann always left on the pretext of having some urgent work to do, because for a workaholic like him any time spent relaxing was time wasted. Eva Braun, on the other hand, was very active and adored walking. Immediately after lunch she rushed off to change and came back accompanied by her friend Herta and her two black terriers. She regularly made a long detour through the woods before joining the other guests.

For his walk the Führer used to wear a large, soft, peaked cap, the only one he had that didn't look like a saucepan dumped straight on his head. He put on a black raincoat or a trenchcoat over his uniform, took a stick and his dog's leash, and set out with one of his guests. The rest of the group followed the same path in random order. Generally the Führer walked slowly, holding Blondi on the leash because that part of the forest was a paradise for game. Roe deer, hares and squirrels leaped about without paying any attention to the walkers. They were used to human beings, and had learnt that no harm would come to them; they also knew that people brought them food in the winter.

Eva's two little dogs sometimes ran through the tall grass of the hillside barking furiously, but the roe deer just gave them a condescending look and ran off with a quick bound only when the dogs came too close.

The tea house stood on a rocky plateau which fell abruptly away to the north, making a natural observation point. Far below flowed the river Ach, which meandered slowly through the valley. Along its banks the houses looked like tiny matchboxes. From here the view stretched as far as Salzburg; only the mountains of the Steinernes Meer hid the view to the left. But the vast rock on which the tea house had been built was worth a visit in itself.

In fine weather, the first arrivals sat outside on a wooden bench to wait for the rest of the party. Eva would have her still camera or her 8mm ciné camera ready to try to catch the Führer. She was the only person who was allowed to photograph him without warning, but it was very difficult to find the right moment. He wanted to be photographed without giving the impression of having posed for the picture, but even when the sky was clear and blue he wore the peaked cap which threw a shadow on his face, and nothing and nobody – not even Eva – could persuade him to take it off. Quite often he also wore sunglasses because of his sensitive eyes. But Eva adored photography, and she was so patient that she managed to get some successful pictures, better even than the photos taken by her old boss Heinrich Hoffmann, who had become the Führer's official photographer.

The tea house was built of rounded stones and was hideous from the outside: it looked like a silo or an electricity installation. Inside, apart from the hall, the kitchen and the guard room, there was a large circular room which could also be reached from the outside through an antechamber furnished with floral-covered armchairs.

The big round room was an architectural masterpiece. The ceiling was lightly vaulted, the walls covered with marble and framed with thin strips of gold. One wall was taken up by six large windows that gave a magnificent view of the surrounding countryside. There was a huge fireplace where a log fire was always burning. The main piece of furniture was a low circular table in the centre of the room, with about twenty padded seats around it covered in beige and red fabric. Near the fireplace stood four enormous armchairs with high backs for the use of the Führer and his guests of honour.

The staff were always forewarned about the arrival of Hitler and his guests, and even before one went inside the house one could smell coffee. The table was laid, and we were served immediately. Eva Braun took her place on Hitler's left, while Frau Schneider sat on his right; the others could sit as they liked. After the walk through the woods everyone was glad to have a cup of coffee or tea, apart from Hitler who stayed faithful to his infusion of apple peel or his cumin tea – nothing else. He'd eat some hot apple strudel and a few diet biscuits. For the guests there were plain cakes and petits fours brought from a cake shop in Berchtesgaden, not always wonderfully fresh.

Conversation was quite difficult. To be heard by everybody one had to speak very loudly, so exchanges were on the whole limited to one-to-one dialogues – but Eva managed to keep the atmosphere friendly with her charm and good humour. She made every effort to take Hitler's mind off the war by talking about plays or films she'd seen. She even tried to convince Hitler to see the films she thought especially good.

'Look,' she said, 'you could have them shown here in the hall. Cinema is an art, it isn't just entertainment. You listen to records, after all. I don't think a single German would see anything wrong in their Führer watching a film now and again – and I'm sure they'd rather your colleagues went to the cinema instead of using official vehicles to go off drinking in bars.'

But Hitler always gave the same reply. 'While the war is on and people are making enormous sacrifices, and I have to shoulder my responsibilities to the end, I just can't allow myself to spend time watching films. Besides, I have to be careful of my eyesight.'

Eva quickly changed the subject. 'In the antechamber I saw some wonderful llama wool blankets,' she said. 'They'd make a beautiful coat. My dressmaker has a pattern which would suit that material perfectly.'

'Those belong to Bormann,' Hitler replied. Here Martin Bormann was still all-powerful, like the Rübezahl, the legendary bad spirit of the mountain. He was responsible for the management of the Platterhof region and the complex of buildings that included the Berghof. He also had responsibility for all the technical installations, the building works and the enormous anti-aircraft defences. Close to the Berghof he had created a model farm which raised pigs and horses; there was a huge orchard with an apple juice factory as well. Although Bormann could sometimes seem jovial and good-natured, that didn't make him any less hated and feared. Eva Braun never got those blankets for her coat.

Hitler always maintained he slept very badly and that if there wasn't absolute silence he found it impossible to sleep. None the less, almost as soon as he'd eaten his last slice of apple strudel and finished his last cup of infusion he shut his eyes, usually on the pretext that the light was too strong, and fell asleep. No one took any notice. The conversation continued quietly. Eva Braun would turn to the other guests or to the person sitting on her left. The young aides-de-camp would melt away, citing urgent telephone calls as an excuse, but actually it was so that they could at last smoke a cigarette. Admiral von Puttkammer, the naval aide-de-camp who was seldom seen without a cigar in his mouth, used to escape to the kitchen and instantly disappear in a cloud of smoke surrounded by all the guards.

Hitler often woke very suddenly, his eyes wide open, and took part in the conversation just as if he'd only lowered his eyelids to relax and think for a moment. Nobody challenged this pretence and he'd ask, 'Schaub, what time is it?' Schaub, who'd been counting the minutes until we could leave, didn't even need to look at his watch. 'Six o'clock, *mein Führer*. Shall I order the cars?' With a speed no one would have thought him capable of he rushed off on his crippled feet to give the order to move.

In the area surrounding the Berghof Hitler drove about in a special model Volkswagen, which was black with a leather interior. He often sat in front beside the driver, with his valet in the back with Blondi. There were other cars for the guests, but most people preferred to go back on foot. The last days of March, when I arrived in Berchtesgaden, were particularly beautiful and it was a pleasure to breathe the pure mountain air. When we got back to the Berghof Hitler would already be resting before his evening conference. That left everyone a couple of hours of freedom in which we could at last be alone and do what we wanted. I used to write letters or go down to Berchtesgaden to visit friends stationed there.

Eva Braun often took advantage of this time to invite members of Hitler's entourage to watch the films she'd taken with her 8mm ciné camera, and sometimes she arranged showings of feature films for all the Berghof staff in a basement room which was in fact a skittle alley. We got the chance to see foreign films which weren't shown to the public, and the GHQ used to be sent German films straight from the Ministry of Propaganda before they'd been examined by the censor. Some of these never went before the general public either.

About seven o'clock the noise of cars coming and going began again, and the whole Berghof came alive. Hitler began his evening briefing session, and, as before, paid absolutely no attention to the time it ended, which was sometimes very late. In the spring of 1943, though, the situation in the various theatres of operations wasn't as serious as it became later, so we could hope that they might be finished by about ten o'clock at the latest. The dinner guests were informed by telephone what time the meal would be served.

Dinner involved the same ceremony as lunch. The dining room slowly filled with men mostly in civilian clothes, and women in their most lavish dresses. It was difficult for me to compete with the standard of elegance, because before the war I rarely had the opportunity to dress up and my wardrobe consisted almost entirely of casual clothes. Even though we didn't wear long evening dresses at the Berghof – luckily – Eva Braun was a fashion parade in herself. She hardly ever wore the same dress twice, even if we stayed there for weeks, and she never appeared in the same outfit at lunchtime, at teatime or in the evening. I admired her taste and her ability to show off her natural elegance to best advantage. She preferred dark colours and loved wearing black. Hitler's favourite dress of Eva's was a sleeveless black one in heavy silk with a wide bell skirt, a very tight waist and two broad rose-coloured bands running down from the shoulders to form a low square neckline, with two roses in the same colour at the corners. On top she wore a short bolero jacket with very narrow long sleeves.

I remember Hitler having rather peculiar opinions about women's fashions. Eva's clothes and her appearance were her consuming passion: she couldn't have endured opening her wardrobe if it hadn't always been full of new dresses. Hitler let her do as she wanted, but he was in the habit of saying, 'I can't understand why you women have to change your clothes all the time. When I like a dress, I want to see it as often as possible. I think a woman should have all her clothes made of the same material and in the same style. As soon as I've got used to something pretty and haven't had time to look at it often enough, you're wearing something new.'

In the same way, Eva wasn't supposed to change her hairstyle. One day she appeared with her hair slightly darker; another time, she had a style that was higher on top of her head. Hitler was bitterly disappointed. 'You look like a stranger. You've become a completely different woman.' Eva rushed away and came back with her usual hairdo.

Hitler also liked making comments about the appearance of other women, approving or criticising the way they looked. Usually he disliked any change, but Frau Schneider, who came in one day with her hair up, provoked an enthusiastic reaction from him. He liked the new image.

Dinner was much the same as the midday meal. We often had cold meat with salad, then a dish called *Hoppelpoppel* which consisted of roast potatoes with eggs and meat; or perhaps we would have noodles with tomato sauce and grated cheese. Hitler almost always ate two fried eggs with creamed potato and salad. Vegetables and fresh fruit were delivered all year round from the glasshouses on Martin Bormann's model farm. He supplied vegetables to the Führer's GHQ even when they had to be flown from Bavaria to East Prussia. Hitler claimed that his fragile digestion meant he could only eat fresh produce, and he didn't like anything to come from foreign suppliers. Naturally, at the Wolfsschanze these deliveries from the farm at Obersalzberg were kept for Hitler himself, but at the Berghof everyone could eat cucumbers, radishes, mushrooms, salads and all sorts of early vegetables from March onwards.

Hitler ate fast and fairly greedily. Once when I was sitting opposite him I saw him watching me as I was helping myself to food. 'You always eat too little, my dear, and anyway you're too thin.' Eva Braun looked at me with contempt, because compared to her I was the image of the typical Bavarian girl, heavy and inelegant. Hitler took the opportunity to return to his hobby-horse about fashion and weight. 'I can't see the attraction of a woman who looks like a boy,' he said. 'We like women because they're different from men. In my day the ballet was a visual treat because you could still see pretty bodies with nice round curves – now all you see is a lot of skeletons jumping about the stage. Goebbels is always trying to drag me along to the ballet, and I've been two or three times. I was very disappointed – but at least I don't have to pay now I'm the Führer; I get free tickets.'

As the meal reached its end the aides-de-camp got up from their places to greet the officers who had arrived for the next working session. When Günsche appeared and announced that everything was ready, Hitler got up and said, 'Please stay where you are. I'll be back to join you shortly.' Then he walked off, his head bowed, his shoulders slightly hunched, but with a firm step.

He wanted to avoid any contact between his guests, especially the ladies, and the military personnel. At the Berghof he led a double life: he was the attentive host, the country house owner who'd come to relax; and at the same time he was the head of state and military chief who was directing the war in all its different theatres of operation. But it was sometimes hard, if only because of the layout of the rooms, to keep the two apart: the house wasn't divided into two sections, one private, the other official. Hitler's office was in the same corridor as Eva Braun's bedroom, for example. It was necessary, therefore, to tell guests who wanted to go to their rooms to avoid the place where an important meeting was taking place.

We were free to occupy our time as we wished for as long as the conference lasted. The day I first lunched with Hitler he had asked us to wait for him as he left the dining room, saying the meeting would be a short one; from this we gathered that neither Goering nor any of the other most senior figures would be there. This was also taken as a sign that the general situation on the various fronts was reasonably satisfactory. Fräulein Schroeder and I, who were on duty, went off to the aides-de-camp's office to deal with any current work – which usually meant making copies of a large number of communiqués about air attacks coming in over the teleprinter from every corner of the country, all of which had to be made legible for the Führer.

On days when there was enough time between the walk to the tea house and dinner, Eva Braun asked for the list of new films and enlisted the other women to help her choose one to watch in the skittle alley. She asked the orderlies to warn her as soon as the conference was over, and then the little group of eight or ten people would head for the basement for their private film show. The kitchen staff and various soldiers often went as well. With a bit of luck we could watch the whole film, but the showing was sometimes interrupted by a telephone call to say that the working session was over and Hitler was waiting for us in the great hall.

The projector was switched off straightaway. Eva Braun would rush off to her room to redo her make-up, and her sister Gretl used to find a quiet corner and smoke one last cigarette before sucking a mint to take away the smell. Everyone gradually congregated in the living room. A baroque lamp was shining over a low table, and in the corner Frau Speer, Frau Bormann and Frau Brandt would often be sitting on a sofa discussing the problems of their children's education. The curtain between the living room and the hall would still be drawn, because Hitler was always delayed after the meeting by someone who had one last request to put to him or an urgent problem to discuss.

It was often midnight by the time Hitler drew back the curtain and appeared in the living room, and then we still had to wait for Eva and her sister. The Führer took all his guests into the great hall. It was the moment for chatting round the fire, and the big sofas and comfortable low chairs had been drawn up to a round table with small occasional tables at the sides. The opposite corner was lit by a standard lamp; on the mantelpiece and in the centre of the big table candles were burning. The shadowy faces of the guests, almost always the same faces, became blurred and hardly recognisable. Hitler himself sat on the right of the fireplace, in the half-darkness; beside him Eva Braun was usually slumped deep in an armchair, her legs stretched out and resting on a stool. The other guests sat where they pleased, without worrying about protocol. Somewhere under the table, or by the fire, lay Negus and Stasi, looking like fat balls of black wool. The dogs of the lady of the house had precedence here, but sometimes Hitler would ask timidly whether he could bring in Blondi, whom they didn't like, for a little while. Then Eva would take her dogs out so that Blondi could come in.

In the evening Hitler drank his usual cumin tea, but alcohol wasn't forbidden and everyone else could drink whatever they wanted: wine, champagne, cognac. There were cakes for us and, for Hitler, his favourite apple strudel. Occasionally Eva Braun managed to persuade the Führer that a few sandwiches would be better than sweet cakes so late at night.

The low lights, the thick carpet which muffled any sound of footsteps and the spluttering logs in the fireplace tended to make everyone fall silent. Hitler wanted to escape his thoughts, to forget what was on his mind. He liked to chat to his neighbour in a low voice, but when this happened to be Frau Bormann, for instance, there was very little to talk about. A quiet woman at the best of times, she couldn't talk to the Führer about her problems with her husband, or the large number of children she'd brought into the world since her marriage to the Reichsleiter. Every spring, when we moved to Obersalzberg, there she was devotedly and patiently clutching another baby to her breast. Pale, insignificant, with thick tresses of hair rolled around her head and ill at ease in the midst of those stylish women, she sat in her armchair beside the Führer and seemed to be counting the minutes until she could at last go to bed.

Another regular guest was Professor Blaschke, Hitler's dentist. He was a sturdy sixty-year-old, who looked the very picture of a learned man with his greying temples, bushy, dense black eyebrows and carefully tended moustache standing out in contrast with his pale face. He was a silent, reserved man, but during those evenings around the fire he was sometimes drawn into conversation by Hitler. Then he showed himself to be one of the few who dared defend his own point of view firmly, even when it differed from Hitler's own.

Like the Führer, Professor Blaschke was a convinced vegetarian, but for different reasons. He claimed that human beings' teeth were designed for a diet based on fruit and vegetables, and that this also suited the human digestive system. But Blaschke occasionally made an exception and ate some meat, especially chicken, which he didn't consider as harmful as red meat.

However when Hitler tried to convince us all, in front of Blaschke, that tobacco was very bad for the teeth, he encountered the stomatologist's most staunch opposition. Blaschke adored smoking, and, perhaps for that reason, was rather more tolerant of it than he should have been from a strictly medical point of view. He even claimed that cigarette smoke had a beneficial effect, acting as a disinfectant for the mouth and regularising the irrigation of the blood vessels. In normal quantities, therefore, smoking wasn't harmful. Hitler, of course, wouldn't hear a word of this. 'Smoking is one of the most dangerous addictions,' he said. 'I find the smell of cigars and cigarettes absolutely horrible, and I'd never offer a cigarette to anyone I liked or respected because I'd be doing something terrible to them. It's proven beyond any possible doubt that non-smokers live much longer than smokers, and that they're much more resistant to disease.'

On hearing that, Gretl Braun declared that she wouldn't want to live a long time if she couldn't smoke, because life wouldn't be so good. 'Besides,' she added, 'I enjoy excellent health even though I've smoked for years.'

'Yes, Gretl,' Hitler replied, 'but your health would be even better if you didn't smoke. And if you get married one day you'll probably find you can't have children. Anyway, the smell of tobacco makes women very unattractive. One day I was at a reception in Vienna and I was sitting next to the great Viennese actress Maria Holst, a woman of real beauty. She had wonderful chestnut hair, but when I leaned towards her her hair gave off a terrible smell of nicotine.'

Whenever Hitler claimed that alcohol was less noxious than nicotine he roused unanimous opposition from all the many smokers in his entourage. My reply was: 'Sir, alcohol can ruin marriages. It can lead to divorce, and it's certainly the cause of lots of traffic accidents. But nicotine can only do a bit of harm to the health of the person who smokes.'

But he wasn't swayed by our arguments, and he'd given orders that in the Christmas parcels sent in his name to the Leibstandarte troops there should be bottles of schnapps but no cigarettes. We didn't miss the opportunity of reminding him that the soldiers would simply swap their chocolates for tobacco or cigarettes, but that didn't make him change his mind. Anyway, Himmler had decided to send packets of cigarettes to his SS troops on his own initiative: he thought that lack of tobacco could have a negative effect on their will to fight.

Hitler delighted in these night-time gatherings. 'I never take holidays, I can't go anywhere to relax, so my holidays are the hours I spend here, beside the fire, with my guests.' He loved the great hall and its fine pictures. He used to stand admiring the painting by Feuerbach and say, 'Doesn't *Nana* look marvellous? It's in the perfect place, above the mantelpiece. Her hands are luminous, so full of life. After my death I'm going to leave all these pictures to a new gallery in Linz. I shall transform Linz into a beautiful great town and I'll give it an art gallery that people will come from far and wide to see. I think of the pictures on my walls as a loan. They make my life more agreeable. When I'm dead, they'll belong to the people of Germany.'

This idea of Hitler's was already well known. He had a deep affection for the town of Linz, where he'd spent his childhood and part of his adolescence. He dreamed of making it the future artistic capital of Europe, and he'd drawn countless sketches and plans for pompous, neo-classical buildings. It was one of the things he liked to talk about with Albert Speer who had originally been one of the Führer's architects. Hitler detested Vienna, which was then the cultural capital of central Europe; possibly he even thought Linz – which was nothing but a modest provincial town – could take its place.

In the evenings, Dr Morell would begin to doze off as soon as he'd had his first glass of port. He fought desperately to stay awake, his fat hairy arms folded over his prominent stomach, but in vain. He had the most peculiar way of shutting his eyes: his bottom lids came up to meet the top ones. He was a horrible sight, with his fishy eyes behind thick spectacles. From time to time Colonel von Below would give him a dig in the ribs, and he'd wake up and immediately give a broad smile, thinking that Hitler must have told a funny story.

'Are you tired, Morell?' the Führer used to ask, to which he'd always reply, 'No, *mein Führer*, I was just thinking.' Then he'd launch into an anecdote about the time he was doctor on board a ship off Africa, to prove he hadn't been asleep.

Eva Braun made great efforts to maintain a relaxed atmosphere. She often led the conversation round to the cinema and the new films she wanted to have shown at the Berghof. Hitler was much less keen than she was, but she did manage to persuade him to watch one of her favourite films, *Gone with the Wind*.

Once Hitler started to whistle a tune he liked. 'That's not right,' Eva said. 'This is how it goes.' She whistled the tune as she thought it should be, but Hitler insisted that his version was correct.

'I bet you I'm right,' she said.

'You know I never make bets with you,' Hitler answered, turning to the rest of us. 'Anyway, I always have to pay up. If I win, I have to give in out of politeness. If she wins, I have to pay the debt.'

'Well, let's listen to the record. You'll see which of us is right,' Eva suggested.

The aide-de-camp, Albert Bormann, found the record and put it on the turntable. Eva turned out to be right, but Hitler wouldn't admit that he was beaten: 'You're right,' he said, 'but the composer was wrong. If he'd been as talented as me, he'd have written my version.'

Everyone laughed, but I wasn't sure that Hitler was joking. He was convinced that his musical ear was infallible. Heinz Lorenz said to him, 'You ought to organise a concert here, in the hall, sir. You could invite all the most famous artistes – Gieseking, Kempff, Furtwängler. You never go to the theatre or to the opera these days, but you could still listen to some music. . . .'

'No,' Hitler replied, 'I couldn't make the musicians go to all that trouble just for me. We can play records.' There was a rack with all the Führer's favourite records in it, several hundred of them, each one numbered. The rack, together with the record player, emerged from a large piece of furniture built into the wall. Bormann operated the record player, and Hitler always chose the same repertoire: operettas by Franz Lehar, songs by Richard Strauss, Hugo Wolf and Richard Wagner. The only popular song was the 'Donkey Serenade', which usually ended the concert.

However, Hitler's colleagues appreciated the music less than the conversations round the fire. One by one they slipped out of the room, and their muffled laughter could be heard in the next room where they were entertaining themselves as they liked, while the boss sat alone with the somnolent Dr Morell, the faithful Eva, the aides-de-camp, Frau von Below and Brandt for company. I must confess that I sometimes crept out discreetly with the others, but the valet often came to find us and said, 'The Führer is missing your company, and besides, the noise coming from this room is distracting to the people listening to the music.' And the faithful had to go reluctantly back to their posts.

Hitler was resigned to this behaviour. 'My entourage certainly isn't very musical,' he used to complain. 'When I'm invited to a gala performance, I have to keep an eye on all the people who accompany me to see they don't fall asleep. Hoffmann almost fell out of the official box during a performance of *Tristan and Isolde*, and I had to wake up Schaub and tell him to shake Hoffmann. Meanwhile, Brückner [an aide] was snoring behind me – it was horrible. Luckily, when it's *The Merry Widow* nobody goes to sleep because there's some ballet in it.'

I once asked the Führer why he always went to hear *The Mastersingers* or another Wagner opera. 'That's just my bad luck,' he replied. 'If ever I say I like a particular opera or a certain bit of music, I'm condemned to hearing it all the time. I once mentioned that I thought *The Mastersingers* was Wagner's finest opera, and since then everyone has assumed it is my favourite. I'm fated to hear it again and again.'

Time went by. On that first occasion it was four o'clock in the morning, or perhaps even later, when Hitler finally called the valet to ask if any air attacks had been reported. He asked this question every night before going to bed, and never retired before he'd made sure that there was no wave of enemy aircraft expected over the territory of the Reich. His informants avoided telling him about isolated incidents or any flights that weren't very important. At long last he got up, shook everyone by the hand and took himself off to his first-floor apartments.

The living room was instantly filled with a dense cloud of cigarette smoke and the atmosphere of boredom gave way to a good-humoured excitement. The countless cups of coffee we'd drunk to help us stay awake meant that we couldn't go to sleep straightaway in any case, and the guests dispersed slowly to their rooms. The Berghof was eventually plunged into a deep silence which lasted until noon the following day.

9

'When will this war be over?'

This was the way I usually spent my days and nights during the first few weeks of my stay at the Berghof. Hitler did not dictate any letters or speeches, as I was expecting. Besides the usual office routine with the aides-de-camp, the secretaries had only social duties.

New guests arrived all the time: Esser, the Minister of State, came for several days with his wife; Baldur von Schirach, the former head of the Hitler Youth and now *Gauleiter* of Vienna, and his wife came, as did Frau Morell and Frau Dietrich, the wife of the Chief Press Officer. Heinrich Hoffmann, the photographer, and Marion Schönmann, a friend of Eva Braun's, were often invited, and Hitler's close colleagues were delighted to see new faces on the daily walks or at the sacred teatime ceremonies.

Hitler envied guests who wore civilian clothes. 'You're lucky,' he said one sunny day to Brandt, who had appeared in a pair of Bavarian *Lederhosen*. 'I used to dress like that all the time.'

'But you could dress like this now, sir. You're a private person here.'

'No – as long as the war lasts, I'll wear my uniform. Anyway, my knees are all white – they'd look terrible in shorts.' And he went on, 'But after the war I'll hang up my uniform, retire to this house and leave all the affairs of state to someone else. When I get old I'll write my memoirs, surrounded only by educated, witty people – no more army officers. They're all empty-headed, dull and stubborn. My two oldest secretaries will stay with me, typing out my memoirs. The young ones will leave to get married, but when I'm old the older ones will be quite happy working at my pace.'

Hearing him say this, I plucked up the courage to ask, 'When will this war be over?'

'I don't know. As soon as we win it!' came the immediate reply. His smiling and kindly expression had given way to the hard fanaticism portrayed on the bronze statues. Hitler rarely spoke of the war in our presence, and said very little about politics. 'We're going to win this war because we're fighting for an ideal, and not for Jewish capitalism like the enemy troops. Russia is the only one of our opponents who is dangerous, because the Russians fight with the same fanaticism as we do for their *Weltanschauung*, their world view. But Right will conquer, that's for certain.'

None of his audience voiced any objections. There were no military personnel present and the civilians believed what Hitler said because they wanted to believe it. A strength that neither men nor women could resist emanated from him. As a man he was modest and amiable; as a Führer he was iron-hard and in the grip of a *folie de grandeur;* he lived his 'mission' with fierce intensity. Sometimes he felt it meant unreasonable sacrifices on his part: 'If you knew how I long simply to walk through the streets, alone, unrecognized and without an escort, just for once! I'd love to be able to go into a shop and buy Christmas presents, or sit in a café and watch the people around me. But I can't!'

We'd say, 'But you could! In the past, kings and emperors have managed to mix with their people. You could put on dark glasses and an ordinary civilian suit, and no one would recognize you.'

'I wouldn't want all that play-acting – and anyway, they'd still recognize me. I'm much too well known and my voice would give me away.'

So, even though he always claimed he wasn't at all worried about an attempt on his life, and the only fear he had about driving through big crowds was that a child might fall under the wheels of his car, he still didn't want to risk being recognized anywhere when he was alone. What he meant was that the inevitable demonstrations of popular affection would spoil his enjoyment of an outing.

For quite a long time Hitler had managed to avoid demonstrations of enthusiasm on the part of the public. For obvious reasons of security the whereabouts of his GHQ was unknown to most people, and his brief stays in Berlin were also kept secret. In the past, the swastika used to be raised over the Reich Chancellery whenever the Führer was in the capital, and it was possible to watch the usual comings and goings of the large official cars. But for the last few years only the initiated few knew that, for instance, the doubling of guards at the front gate meant that the Führer was in the Chancellery. Even when he travelled in his special train everything was done to hide his presence: the windows of his carriage were blacked out in broad daylight as well as at night, and Hitler spent his days in artificial light, as he did later on in his bunker.

At the Berghof, in the old days, the crowds used to form a human wall around the last gate out of Berchtesgaden before the mountain road that led to Hitler's residence; now there was no one to be seen. Before the war, when Hitler went out for a walk the gates were opened and the crowd rushed to follow in his path. Hysterical women picked up stones he'd trodden on as souvenirs, and the most reasonable of people behaved like lunatics. Once a delivery man carrying a load of fabric destined for the Berghof was stopped by some over-excited women who carried off the material – which hadn't even been touched by the Führer – like precious trophies, to decorate the windows of their living rooms. The majority of the letters addressed to the Führer at the Chancellery came from women of that sort.

By 1943, however, Hitler spent his time at the Berghof surrounded only by his few close friends and his permanent colleagues. He had a great liking for the architect Albert Speer, whom he'd made Minister of Armaments. 'He's an artist,' Hitler used to say, 'and so his soul is close to mine. I have the warmest human relationship with him because I understand him so well. . . . Like me, he's an architect, intelligent and modest, and has nothing in common with those bull-headed military men. I never imagined he'd master his enormous job so well. He also has great gifts as an organizer; he's absolutely on top of his work.'

It's true that Speer was a pleasant man. He wasn't in any way a party man or a pushy *arriviste*, but a competent professional who never stooped to saying 'Yes' against his better judgement. He was one of the few people from whom the Führer would accept any contradiction or alternative opinion. Hitler once said, 'When I give Speer a plan to execute, he considers it for a while and then says "Yes sir, I think it's feasible," but he sometimes also says, "No, it won't work like this." And his arguments always hold water.'

Speer wore uniform, since he held a public position, but he always looked relaxed and there was nothing the least bit military about him. His hair was always a little too long, but he didn't notice until his wife pointed it out to him. I never saw him drunk

76

and he never took part in any celebrations with Hitler's entourage. Neither did I ever notice that he was at all friendly with the party men or the Wehrmacht.

Heinrich Hoffmann was the very opposite of Speer. He was a veteran from the 'time of combat', invariably there with his camera wherever Hitler appeared. It was in recognition of this indefatigable devotion to his work that he'd been awarded the title 'Professor', although I always wondered what talent he had that justified it. His business acumen? Or perhaps the opportunism that led him to choose, out of the thirty political parties of the time, to devote his photographic talents exclusively to the National Socialists. He was also a talented draughtsman, and he could be witty at times, but he was a very unlikeable man.

Hitler's friendship for Hoffmann led him to be extremely indulgent. Although he wouldn't think twice about dismissing or demoting a colleague or any of his generals who dared to contradict him, he was ready to excuse any number of faults or personal weaknesses in his old comrades, even when their behaviour was much more harmful to the working of the party or the ideal of National Socialism than openly expressed disagreement would have been. Hitler was shocked by Hoffmann's immoderate use of alcohol and his reputation with women, but he seemed to turn a blind eye to the orgies the 'Professor' held in Vienna, in Munich and in his country house at Altötting, which scandalized his neighbours. And who could say anything against a friend of the Führer's? Eva Braun was the only person who tried. 'You must do something,' she said. 'Hoffmann behaves appallingly badly. He's always drunk and he throws lavish parties at a time when most people have practically nothing to eat.'

That would make Hitler angry, certainly, and he'd chastise Hoffmann – but without any lasting effect. And he was always trying to find excuses for his friend: 'The death of his first wife affected him very badly. He's never got over it. That's when he began to drink. Before her death he was a marvellous husband.'

In fact, the faithful comrade had never been averse to a good bottle of wine, and Hitler himself used to tell stories about it. One was the tale of a car journey he'd made with Hoffmann in the 1920s.

'Hoffmann had bought a new car, a Ford, and insisted I try it out with him. I said, "No, Hoffmann, I'm not getting into a car with you!" but he nagged at me until I agreed. We started off in the Schellingstrasse (where the party newspaper was produced).

It was evening, and it was raining. Hoffmann set off through the streets like a madman, almost crashed into a house and paid no attention at all to pedestrian crossings. I shouted at him, "Hoffmann, you're driving like a maniac, you're going to kill us both!"

' "No, no, sir – you only think that because you haven't had anything to drink. If you'd had a good glass of red wine like me, you wouldn't notice a thing!"

'At that point I got out of the car, and that was the last time I let myself be driven by him.'

Since the beginning of the war, Hoffmann had had fewer and fewer occasions to see the Führer. There was nothing for him to do at GHQ, and the only place he could see him was at the Berghof. At first, Hitler felt very pleased when his faithful old companion arrived after months of absence, but Hoffmann quickly got on his nerves. He used to tease him about his drinking. 'Hoffmann, your nose looks like a gourd. If we lit your breath with a match you'd explode.' 'Soon there won't be any blood flowing in your veins – it'll be neat red wine,' he said one day when Hoffmann appeared at lunch already drunk. Finally Hitler enlisted the help of Julius Schaub and Martin Bormann: 'Please try to make sure the Professor turns up sober. I invited him here so that I could enjoy his company, and he shouldn't be drinking like this.' From that moment onwards, Hoffmann couldn't find a single person willing to have a drink with him, and in the end he took to carrying around his own bottle. By then he irritated Hitler so much that he was only asked to the Berghof on very rare occasions.

However, he could still entertain Hitler and the other guests with his conversation. 'Sir, here's a riddle for you. Himmler, Goering and you are walking along the street with only one umbrella among you. Which of the three gets wet?' Nobody knew the answer. 'None of you, because it's not raining!'

Hitler shook his head, 'Poor old Hoffmann, you're beginning to show your age.'

Everyone laughed, but Hoffmann added, 'And just think, the person who told me that joke is in Dachau now.'

'That's ridiculous,' the Führer said. 'The story's too silly.'

'Oh yes, really. He's in Dachau because that's where he lives.' Hoffmann looked triumphant, and Hitler laughed.

Around the fire in the evenings, they had long conversations about the art gallery and about the painting exhibitions that

Hoffmann organized in the Haus der Deutschen Kunst (House of German Art), a new building erected by Hitler in Munich which received annual donations of the work of painters and sculptors who lived up to the canons of Nazi art. Everyone else got very bored during these conversations, but Hoffmann was well aware of Hitler's love of painting and his particular tastes, especially for the old masters.

Hoffmann's daughter, Frau Henrietta von Schirach, was once among the guests. She was a nice Viennese woman, very unaffected and full of life, but she had to cut short her visit because she caused an incident one teatime. I wasn't there at the time, but it was told to me by Hans Junge, who was one of Hitler's duty valets that day. When Hitler was chatting to his guests, she suddenly said, *'Mein Führer*, when I was in Vienna I saw a trainload of Jews being deported. It was terrible . . . those poor people looked so miserable. Do you know this is happening, and do you allow it?' A deathly silence followed her question, and soon afterwards Hitler got up and left. The next morning Frau von Schirach went back to Vienna and she did not come to the Berghof again; the incident was never mentioned.

In the first few days of April 1943, Hitler felt sufficiently rested and began preparations for visits from friendly heads of state. Ribbentrop, the Minister of Foreign Affairs, came for meetings and stayed to lunch almost every day. The busiest person was Ambassador Hewel. Almost all the heads of state of the countries allied to Hitler were due to pay visits to the stunning baroque castle at Klessheim, near Salzburg, which had been built by Fischer von Erlach and wonderfully decorated and furnished according to Hitler's taste. That was where the Führer entertained high-ranking foreigners for whom the Berghof, which was essentially a private house, didn't seem appropriate.

The first and most important of these guests was Mussolini. The evening before his arrival, Hitler was in an unusually good mood. 'The *Duce* is a great statesman,' he said. 'He knows the mentality of his countrymen perfectly, and what he's managed to achieve with Italy, and those lazy people, is a miracle. But his position isn't easy. He's stuck between the Church and the Royal Family. The King is senile, of course, but he has a lot of supporters. Victor Emmanuel is the smallest king I've ever seen. When I went to Rome in my private train in 1938, I warned my staff, when we were about to arrive at the station, that if they saw on the platform a tiny little man in uniform covered with bits of gold and medals, they shouldn't laugh – it'd be the King of Italy, who never managed to grow any taller.

'Of course my men, who were all very tall, might easily have burst out laughing, because he was a grotesque sight. When the King and Queen – she was at least two feet taller than him – were sitting side by side at table they looked as if they were more or less the same height, but as soon as he got up out of his seat the King seemed to shrink and the Queen seemed to get ever taller. . . . Apart from that, Rome was marvellous. Italy is an enchanting country: it's just a pity it's inhabited by such lazy slobs.'

Hitler went on to describe the grandiose demonstrations and lavish receptions the *Duce* had organized in honour of his guests. The Fascist population had produced a most enthusiastic welcome and endless ovations for their friend and ally. Later, after Italy's defection, Hitler decided all these warm demonstrations of affection were 'a flash in the pan', and the Italians 'people with no backbone'.

He had been to the opera with Mussolini, and was horrified by the lack of respect the audience showed towards the performers. 'The women sitting in the boxes and the stalls, all dressed in their sumptuous clothes, were chatting and gossiping amongst themselves while the singers were doing their best to give a good performance. We arrived in the middle of the second act and I couldn't believe my ears when the orchestra stopped, in the middle of the opera, and started to play the Italian and German national anthems and the "Horst Wessel" [a Nazi anthem]. I was really embarrassed: I thought it was so rude to the performers.'

Hitler seemed to feel a deep friendship for Mussolini, and was apparently sincerely pleased about his visit. Perhaps he also hoped for some support from his friend. In any case, he was very skilled at emphasizing his personal feelings.

The day of the great visit was blessed with 'propaganda weather', as we used to call it. The sun, the snow and the blue sky created a perfect setting for the grandiose Klessheim castle. I wasn't aware of what happened at the meeting itself, because I stayed at the Berghof with some other colleagues to get through a backlog of work. A sizeable number of telegrams reporting air attacks had arrived from the Rhineland and northern Germany.

That morning, Eva Braun had set off with her friend Herta Schneider and Frau von Below to walk to a nearby lake, the Königsee, and wouldn't be back until the evening. She was making the most of that free day to go for a long hike, instead of being present at lunch and those interminable hours around the fire – hours which suffocated her and made it impossible for her to enjoy the open-air life she loved.

I was on duty that day, and so wasn't able to leave the Berghof to take advantage of the beautiful weather. Sitting on the terrace, I felt that I was – as the expression goes – trapped in a gilded cage. By that time I'd started to feel uneasy. I couldn't really explain it to myself. It wasn't the mountains oppressing me; rather the powerful machine I'd become part of without realizing it, and which now held me prisoner by so many tentacles.

I was startled out of my thoughts by a telephone call. The Führer had just left Klessheim and wanted to go to the tea house. I changed quickly, thinking I heard the barking of the two Scotch terriers which would announce Eva Braun's return. Shortly afterwards, Hitler and a small group of people set off towards the tea house. I was convinced that the Führer would be tired and silent after a long and busy day full of important business, but the meeting with Mussolini seemed to have pleased him. He was highly excited and talkative, and the evening seemed to last for ever.

Other visits followed: Marshal Antonescu of Romania, Admiral Horthy, Regent of Hungary, and Boris III, King of Bulgaria. On these days we didn't see the Führer until the evening. King Boris was the only guest to come to the Berghof, and I saw him just at the moment when he arrived on the doorstep. I wanted to run to my room but I suddenly found myself in the middle of the procession that had formed to convey the king through the living room into the great hall. I was holding two ping-pong bats in my hands, and my mouth was full because I had just bitten into an apple. Hitler and the king glanced at me in surprise, and I disappeared as fast as I could without even stammering a word of apology. That evening, I apologized to the Führer as soon as he came in to dinner, but he smiled at me: 'That's quite all right, my dear. A king is just a man like any other!'

The official visits were over, but another annual event was in store for us: the Führer's birthday on 20 April. During the weeks that led up to it, mail had arrived by the sackful – letters of congratulation as well as packages and boxes that piled up in Bormann's house. And this was only a small part of the total, because most of the presents were addressed to Berlin. Countless factories and companies, party organizations, schools, syndicates and private individuals sent the most varied and unexpected presents, together with their birthday wishes. There were tooth-brushes and complete outfits of children's clothes, ladies' lingerie, costly porcelain and objects of museum quality. Most of the presents weren't intended for Hitler's own use, of course, but for distribution to people in need. He also received some touching offerings from very humble people. One old woman had made him a pair of slippers embroidered with a swastika over a setting sun, which must have been a great deal of work for her even though they were in the worst possible taste. Another woman sent a large handkerchief whose four corners were embroidered with the faces of Hitler, Hindenburg, Bismarck and Frederick the Great, assembled to wipe the Führer's nose! Cakes, tarts, sweets and fruit also arrived from every corner of Germany. The aides-de-camp's offices looked like a huge bazaar. Letters and presents from the Führer's personal friends and relatives were taken to his office unopened.

At the end of the day on 19 April we were all gathered around the great fireplace. The evening passed as usual. Hitler talked at length about his beloved Blondi, who was allowed to be present for once. I love dogs, and was very impressed by her intelligence. She'd been taught to sit up and beg, of course, and to play 'good pupil', sitting on her back legs with her front paws resting on the arm of her master's chair like an attentive schoolgirl. But her party piece was singing. Hitler would say: 'Blondi, sing to us!' in his most coaxing voice, and let out a long howl himself. She would start on a sharp note and her 'song' would become more and more high-pitched as Hitler encouraged her. If she reached a point that was too shrill, he'd say: 'Sing lower, Blondi, like Zarah Leander!' and she would give a long, low moan like the wolves she was probably descended from. At the end of the performance she used to be given three pieces of cake, and when Hitler held up three fingers she showed how pleased she was: she knew her reward was coming. Almost the whole evening was devoted to Blondi, as if it were her birthday instead of Hitler's.

The moment when the hands of the clock were just on midnight came at last. The big doors opened and the orderlies and valets came in holding trays laden with glasses of champagne. Each of the guests was served with one, and Hitler was handed a glass of very sweet wine. As the first chime of midnight struck, we gathered round him to raise our glasses and wish him happy birthday. Some of the group confined themselves to wishing him good health and simply said: 'Many happy returns, *mein Führer,*' while others made lengthy toasts full of hopes for a long life in which he might continue to lead the German people. This ceremony ended the official celebration of his birthday; we all went back to our seats and general conversation began again. Later, many other people arrived to present their best wishes – valets and servants, guards, chauffeurs, kitchen staff, the children of friends and acquaintances. There were celebrations in every part of the Berghof, in the garages, offices and guard rooms. That day everyone was allowed to drink as much as they wanted. As for myself, I took advantage of the unusual number of visitors to slip away and get to bed at a reasonable hour for once.

10

The Führer's Fifty-Fourth Birthday

On the morning of 20 April, Hitler appeared earlier than usual. Smiling cheerfully, and occasionally with some astonishment, he examined the mountain of gifts piled up in his office. He kept a few of them for himself – a pretty statuette of a young girl, a wooden cup carved by a fourteen-year-old boy, and some children's drawings he wanted to show Eva. All the rest were to be sent to hospitals or children's homes, and anything edible had to be destroyed in case it was poisoned.

At about noon the guests began to arrive: Himmler and SS General Sepp Dietrich, Goebbels and Esser, Ribbentrop and Inspector General Werlin. The list was so long that there was no space to spare at the round table in the bay window. I was the lady of honour at Himmler's table, and it was the first time I'd been so close to this powerful and much feared man. To begin with, I didn't think he was entirely horrible: he just seemed like a lower middle-class government clerk, a bit of a hypocrite, rather than a brutal monster. He had a disconcerting habit of kissing your hand when greeting you, and he spoke in a low voice with a slight Bavarian accent. There was always a smile in his eyes and hovering at the corners of his mouth, and his manner was engaging and amiable. Remembering his chatty manner and the stories he related, it is impossible for me to equate this with the executions, the way things really were in the concentration camps, and the other horrors I now know he was responsible for.

He was extremely crafty. For instance, he explained the perfect organization he'd instituted in the concentration camps. 'I've individually trained my people to achieve the best and most effective work they're capable of, and, thanks to my methods, the camps are orderly and efficient as well as absolutely secure. So, if there's an incorrigible pyromaniac, he's put in charge of the camp fire brigade. He's responsible for any little fire that might occur, and I make sure he's told that if anything happens he's the first suspect. You can't imagine how conscientious and attentive to his work that makes him!'

When he said this, Himmler laughed with a self-satisfied expression, as if he thought he was giving us the idea that he was concerned about the psychology of the people imprisoned in the camps: not content with keeping them locked up, he was making every effort to reform and re-educate them. Hitler made a small movement of his head to indicate his approval of what Himmler was saying, and nobody else dared give their opinion. At that time, we thought these camps were concentration camps within Germany, the kind that had existed since the mid-1930s for opponents of the regime and common criminals; none of us had heard of the death camps set up in Polish territory from 1941 onwards, where Jews were gassed. The existence of these was top secret.

Ribbentrop was a curious figure. He gave the impression of being absent-minded, constantly lost in thought, and if I hadn't known that he was the Minister of Foreign Affairs for the Reich I'd have taken him for a solitary eccentric. Quite out of the blue, and for no particular reason, he suddenly asked Hitler in the middle of a conversation why he didn't drink champagne: 'It makes you feel extraordinarily refreshed, and it's very easy on the digestion.'

Hitler gave him a surprised glance and told him straight out that he couldn't stand champagne. 'I find it too acid, and when I want to drink something fizzy I prefer a mineral water like Fachinger or Apollinaris. I'm sure it's much healthier.'

Long before becoming the grand master of Third Reich diplomacy Ribbentrop had been a representative for Mumm champagne – something he now preferred to forget. He had an impressive air about him, certainly, but I couldn't forget the gaffe we had heard about: at an official reception at Buckingham Palace he'd greeted the King of England with his arm raised, crying 'Heil Hitler!'

Goebbels always brought a sense of humour and a lively atmosphere to these now routine gatherings. He was far from handsome, but I had begun to understand why the young secretaries at the Reich Chancellery used to run to the windows to catch a glimpse of him as he left the Ministry of Propaganda, when they didn't pay the same attention to Hitler himself. 'Oh, if you saw Goebbels's eyes, and his lovely laugh. . . .' they used to say when I gazed at them in astonishment. The women guests at the Berghof used to flirt with him in the same way. He certainly had a sharp wit, and the kind of irony that pierced its victim with relentless accuracy. There was no one at the Führer's table capable of outwitting him, especially not Dietrich, the Reich's Chief Press Officer. Once Dietrich made the comment, slightly out of context, that all his best ideas came to him in the bathroom. 'You ought to take baths much more often, Dr Dietrich!' was Goebbels's immediate reply.

Regular guests of Hitler's were well aware of the coldness between Goebbels and Himmler. They ignored each other totally. It never went further than that, but everyone noticed that their only relationship was one of strict politeness. In fact, the two men were hardly ever invited at the same time, and their respective functions didn't force them into contact. That was not the case with the mutually antagonistic brothers, Martin and Albert Bormann, whom Hitler kept tied with the same leash. Their animosity had reached the point where they could sit side by side and give the impression that they were complete strangers, and if Hitler gave the 'little' Albert Bormann a letter or a note for his brother the Reichsleiter, the former would leave the room and call an orderly to take it to the latter. When one of the two told an anecdote at table that made everybody laugh, the other brother would sit stony-faced, more unresponsive than ever. Hitler accepted the situation; perhaps he even liked it. I never knew where their animosity sprang from. People used to say it was something to do with a woman, but the two brothers themselves seemed to have forgotten.

On Hitler's birthday tea was served in the great hall, and all the high-ranking military personnel were present – Jodl, Keitel, Schmundt and others. Goering appeared in time for the briefing session and took the opportunity to convey his best wishes to the Führer. At the end of the afternoon his wife, whose nickname was 'The Queen Mother', arrived wearing a vast blue cape and accompanied by her little daugher Edda, who was named after Mussolini's daughter, the wife of Ciano, the Italian Foreign Minister. Eva Braun rushed off to the floor above to fetch her camera, hoping to catch the moment when Edda made her little speech to 'Uncle Hitler'. It was one of the very rare occasions when Hitler was on the terrace bare-headed, without his eternal cap, and Eva wanted to get the picture at all costs. Later on Hitler went to make his traditional visit to the wounded soldiers in the hospital at Platterhof, as he had done on each of his birthdays since the beginning of the war.

That day provided an interesting meeting for me, as I met the person who had been my predecessor as Hitler's secretary and whom he always talked about with great enthusiasm. Before her marriage her name had been Gerda Daranowski; she was now the wife of General Eckard Christian, Head of Operations on the Luftwaffe General Staff. She'd been sad to leave her job with the Führer, but Eva Braun hadn't been sorry because Hitler used to speak of his secretary a bit too warmly. She was dark, well-formed and very chic; she carried herself beautifully and looked very young. The Führer seemed susceptible to her sex appeal as well as appreciating her qualities as a secretary. I'd seldom seen such perfect keyboard work – her hands were exceptionally agile and supple – and later I had the opportunity to work with her when she took up her job with the Führer again during the last miserable days in Berlin.

It was at the Berghof that the habitués of the inner circle began to notice my romance with Hans Junge, with whom I'd got on very well since our first meeting. I used to excuse myself from being present at lunch on the days when Linge was on duty – the days when Hans Junge was free, in other words. We used to set off for long walks in the mountains, or else stroll down to Berchtesgaden or Salzburg. But Julius Schaub, who was insatiably nosy, was always on the lookout for some spicy titbit for Hitler, whom he liked to regale with a new piece of gossip at breakfast time. The Führer enjoyed snippets of gossip about banal flirtations, but he wouldn't stand for any serious relationships in his immediate entourage.

Hans Junge was a special favourite of the Führer's. He served him devotedly, with a strong sense of duty, but none the less liked to keep his distance. He was one of the few who honestly admitted the extent of Hitler's influence, and realized that his own ways of thinking had been completely subsumed by the Führer's. Because he wanted to be able to keep an objective view, he had several times asked to be sent to the Russian front – his only chance of leaving the Führer's personal service. But his request had always been turned down. The reason Hitler gave was always the same: there were plenty of good soldiers but few trustworthy orderlies and aides-de-camp.

Under the circumstances in which we lived and worked, the only way Hans and I could see each other more often and get to know each other better was to get engaged. We decided to tell Hitler our plans, but without rushing into anything. Schaub was in seventh heaven when we asked him to let the Führer know, and, shortly after the birthday celebrations, he relayed the news to his boss. I must admit I found the whole business agonizing. At the next meal I felt Hitler looking at me with a knowing smile, and I thought I sensed spiteful glances coming my way from around the table. I reached the point where I wanted to stand up and disappear. Besides, I remembered having said only three months before, in tones of absolute sincerity, that men didn't interest me at all.

By the fire that evening, Hitler suddenly said, 'I have such bad luck with all my people. First Christian took Dara away to marry her and deprived me of my best secretary, and no sooner do I find the perfect replacement than she wants to leave me and take my best valet with her!' Then, turning to me, he said, 'But you'll stay here with me for the time being anyway, since Junge has his heart set on leaving for the front.'

So there I was, suddenly engaged, and equally suddenly facing this new state of affairs, for which I felt not at all prepared. I thought to myself that the only thing I could do was be optimistic about the future.

Just before 1 May, German National Labour Day, I was summoned to the Führer to take down a text he considered important. In the past he had always addressed huge public meetings in person and taken part in the celebrations and the massive demonstrations. But for the last few years he had recorded his speeches for transmission by radio. Sometimes, his proclamations were read aloud or published in the newspapers. But these days he never spoke in public without a manuscript. 'I'd much rather speak freely, without a script,' he used to say, 'but now that we're at war I'm forced to weigh every word, because the world is listening and it has very sharp ears. If I said a single thing that wasn't absolutely right, even as an off-the-cuff remark, the consequences could be very serious.'

The only times the Führer spoke without a script were in front of a restricted audience, party officials, *Gauleiters* or industrialists. I'd been warned several days in advance that he wanted to dictate an important speech, but it wasn't until the night of 30 April that he felt ready to do so. I typed for hours, and didn't finish until early in the morning; at ten Hitler recorded the speech, and at midday it was broadcast on every radio station.

Not long afterwards, Hitler left for Munich with a small group of close associates. He didn't want to miss the annual exhibition which was opening in July at the Haus der Deutschen Kunst. Since he was due to return to his GHQ in East Prussia in July, Heinrich Hoffmann and the widow of Hitler's chief architect, Professor Troost, had arranged a preview of the selected pictures and sculptures well before the exhibition's opening date.

I was the only woman included in the party. Whenever Hitler went to his Munich home in the Prinzregentenplatz I paid a surprise visit to my mother, but on this occasion the joy of seeing each other again didn't last long, because Schaub very soon summoned me to the Führer's house. I already knew the building, but not his apartment, and I was astonished to find that he only had one floor of the house. The ground floor was occupied by the porter and by various offices for guards and policemen. On the second storey was the apartment Hitler shared with his house-keeper, Frau Winter, and her husband. All the other floors were inhabited by private individuals.

The Führer's apartment was just like any other apartment belonging to a well-to-do bourgeois. In the hall there were pieces of wicker furniture, every window was curtained with flowery material, and the walls of a dressing room were covered in mirrors lit by wall lamps. Everything was in very good taste, and there were thick carpets throughout the apartment. At the end of the corridor, on the left, was a door leading to the rooms where the Winters lived: a kitchen, bathroom, living room and bedroom. This living room doubled as a waiting room for Hitler's ministers when the government was in Munich.

Opposite the front door was the Führer's spacious office and his library. Hitler had a strong preference for large rooms, and later on I often wondered how he could bear living caged up under the low ceilings and tiny windows of his bunker. Next to the library was a bedroom which was kept locked: it was there that his beloved niece Geli Raubal had killed herself. Hitler had been so upset by her death that no one had been allowed to enter the room since it happened. Eva Braun also had a small room at her disposal, but she used it rarely, and never when Hitler was in Munich. The right wing contained a guest room which I used as an office whenever I had some typing to do, and between the two was the bedroom where Hitler slept, which I'd never been into.

He had called me in to dictate a very brief and simple document; I took him a copy in his office a short time later. He was sitting at his desk, and I stood beside him while he read it through and, as always, made a few changes. Suddenly, without looking up, he said, 'I hear you're engaged to Hans Junge. Wouldn't you rather get married straight away, before he goes off to the front?'

I looked at him in astonishment, because we hadn't been planning to get married so soon. I was particularly surprised that he should mention it. I searched quickly for a convincing argument, but I couldn't think of one. I just said, 'But, sir, why should we get married? It wouldn't make any difference, since my fiancé will be leaving for the front very soon, and I'll go on working . . . there's no need for us to get married.'

Secretly I wondered why the Führer was so interested in my marriage. Love isn't an affair of state. This was no one's business but mine, and I felt especially irritated at this intrusion into my private life from on high. I was even more astonished to hear Hitler saying, 'But you love each other, don't you? So it'd be better if you got married straightaway. When you're his wife, I'll be better able to protect you if anyone else bothers you.'

I felt an urge to laugh. This all sounded so petit bourgeois. But I didn't have the courage to tell him that love isn't always enough of a reason for getting married, especially for getting married in such a hurry. So I said nothing, thinking that it wasn't really very important and that he'd probably forget all about it.

When I told Hans what Hitler had said, he burst out laughing. 'That's typical of him,' he said. 'Whenever he sees a chance to marry someone off, he always goes on about it. But don't worry: he probably didn't mean it seriously.' I promised myself that one day I'd ask Hitler why he wasn't married – he claimed to love Eva Braun, after all. But at the time I was too young and too shy to ask a question like that.

In Munich, Hitler used to have lunch in a small restaurant he'd frequented in the past: the Osteria Bavaria, in the Schellingstrasse, close to the printing works where the *Völkischer Beobachter*, the Nazi party newspaper, was produced. The proprietor went by the good Bavarian name of Deutelmoser. He had been warned of our visit, and was dressed in his best when we arrived. Lunchtime was almost over, and only a few late customers were still eating. I wondered whether there were any plain-clothes men amongst them, because I was curious about how the Führer's security arrangements operated. But either they were especially skilful agents, or else they really were genuine customers, because they behaved perfectly normally, gazing curiously at all that was happening at the important person's table and leaving, for the most part, before we did.

The table Hitler usually occupied was the least comfortable in the whole place – right at the back, in a corner. We were a group of six: Hitler and two aides-de-camp, Professor Morell, Frau Troost and myself. Professor Troost had built the Haus der Deutschen Kunst, and Hitler liked his widow a great deal. She herself was an interior decorator and architect, so she was in part following in her husband's footsteps. She used to do the design work on all sorts of projects Hitler commissioned: for example, she had designed the document proclaiming Goering as *Reichsmarschall*, the highest military post in the Reich, and his marshal's baton.

Frau Troost was a woman full of spirit and vitality, both thoughtful and witty. She kept up a lively conversation throughout the whole meal, talking so fast and volubly that Hitler could hardly get in a word. She even made fun of his diet, assuring him that he shouldn't expect to live long if he went on feeding himself on plates of mush instead of a good piece of meat.

The meal did not last long and Hitler went back to his apartment by car. In the afternoon there was a conference in the 'Führer's Building' in the Königplatz, with the political leaders and the *Gauleiters*. My presence was no longer required, so I was able to go home and spend the rest of the day with my mother.

When I arrived at the Berghof two days later, I found out that the Führer had been putting pressure on Hans to arrange a quick wedding. Hans hadn't been able to find any useful arguments to counter with, either; deep down, I think he was pleased. In the end I came to terms with the idea of getting married soon, and we set the date for the middle of June. But I rebelled again when I discovered that I had to fill in certain forms and questionnaires, because I was marrying a member of the SS. I was so angry that I told my future husband I was going to throw them all in the bin if my marriage depended on that. Even Hitler started laughing when I read him some of the questions I was asked: 'Does the wife-to-be enjoy housework?' He realized it was a piece of nonsense, and promised to speak to Himmler about it when he had a chance. I was relieved of the obligation to fight that battle with bureaucracy, and, almost before I had time to realize it, mid-June had arrived and I was Frau Junge.

My conjugal bliss lasted just four weeks. A whistle-stop honeymoon beside Lake Constance, and then my husband left for the front and I went back to the Wolfsschanze.

11

Just Married

In the meantime, Hitler and the entire General Staff had left for the Wolfsschanze in East Prussia. The forest had thinned out considerably, as so many trees had been felled to build chalets and bunkers. What we used to call 'chalet fever' had got much worse, and now extended to all the high-ranking officers – everyone wanted to live in a barrack, separate from the bunker, which had become nothing more than a service dormitory. Speer had had a full-blown cottage built for himself; Goering's was like a small palace; the doctors and the aides-de-camp had set themselves up as if they were in a summer holiday resort and Dr Morell – he was the only one to manage it – had a proper bathroom. Once again he found himself the butt of sarcastic remarks throughout the camp, because everyone realised that a normal-sized bath would be much too small for someone as fat as him. People used to say that he could get into the bath on his own but it was impossible for him to extricate himself again without outside help.

When I returned to the camp, newly married, I presented myself to Hitler on the first morning. He was just about to set off for his walk. 'But you look all pale and thin!' he cried, in a friendly way. Linge, Hewel and Schaub had trouble controlling their urge to giggle, and I blushed as red as a beetroot. From then onwards Hitler no longer called me *Mein Kind*, my child, but *Junge Frau*, young lady.

Whatever else could be said of Hitler's secretaries, they were certainly not overworked. Fräulein Wolf and Fräulein Schroeder, the old guard, worked for Schaub. Every morning he would hand them a small pile of letters, sum up in a few words what the replies should be, and leave them the job of writing the answers.

I was responsible for the office work of three young aides-de-camp: Darges, Günsche and Pfeiffer. The work consisted of communiqués addressed to the forces of the Leibstandarte Adolf Hitler Division, requests for promotion, transfer orders and recommendations for decorations. There were more and more of these, as acts of courage multiplied in the violent fighting on the Eastern Front. Iron Crosses and gold and silver medals were awarded with generosity.

This work didn't fill my days, and I had plenty of time to enjoy the forest and the lake. None the less I felt imprisoned, especially because of the restricted life we led, which I found hard to accept. Perhaps I was too young. Maybe I was also influenced by my husband. I was beginning to grasp the monstrosity of living in a world totally dominated by Hitler's ideas. Until now I'd thought of myself as existing at the heart of the war machine, the place from which all the wires led outwards; here, I thought, one had the most accurate and complete view of events. But I realised that in fact we were in the wings, and couldn't see what was being enacted on the front of the stage. Each person knew his or her own part, but no one knew what parts others were playing: only the director knew the whole play. Here, there weren't even any rumours, no clandestine foreign radio bulletins, no divergent points of view – any hint of opposition was unthinkable. There was only one set of beliefs, and sometimes it seemed that everyone around me had the same views, the same expressions, and even used the same words.

It was only later, after the bitter end to it all, when I returned to a normal life, that I clearly understood this feeling. At the time, I had only a sense of dissatisfaction and a vague fear I couldn't put a name to: daily contact with Hitler prevented me from giving a precise form to my thoughts. I began to keep a diary, as a form of mental stimulation and in the hope of maintaining an objective distance. I spoke of my doubts to the people closest to me, and in several of them I discovered analogous feelings. One in particular was Ambassador Hewel, with whom I sometimes had long conversations in the evenings. He too found it hard to bear the facile and blinkered atmosphere in which we all lived, and the lack of genuine human contact in our environment. We called our state of mind 'camp madness', but that didn't help us to get at the roots of it.

Now that we regularly ate lunch with Hitler at the GHQ I had gradually lost my shyness in his presence, and I had become bold

94

enough to ask him questions even before he spoke to me himself. As far as he was concerned, he was more and more insistent that it was beneficial to him to be able to relax and feel uninhibited during meals. One day I decided to take the opportunity to complain about the lack of work I had to do, and at that Hitler announced to us all that Dara – the abbreviation of her maiden name of Daranowski, which was what he always called her – was coming back to work for him. 'The other day I asked General Christian how his wife was, and he told me she was going to work for the Red Cross. But if she wants to go back to work, she might just as well come back to work for me.' My two colleagues were clearly a bit disappointed by this news, although they managed to greet it with a smile. They had always been rather jealous of Dara, whereas they never thought of me as a rival.

Johanna Wolf and I did our best to explain tactfully that we felt guilty about being nothing but social companions. After all, it was wartime, and most Germans were leading hard lives. Since the Führer had so little need of us, couldn't we be more useful in Berlin, or somewhere else? We met with no success at all. 'Ladies,' Hitler replied. 'It's not up to you to decide whether your work or your presence here is useful or otherwise. Believe me, being on my staff is more important than typing letters in some commercial company or other, or turning out shells in some factory. You're serving your country best during the time you spend dealing with my correspondence or helping me snatch a few moments' relaxation so that I can recoup my strength.'

A few weeks later Frau Christian arrived, accompanied by numerous suitcases and hatboxes. From now on, two of us would be present at lunch with the Führer, and two at dinner. When I was at Hitler's table with her, the conversation sometimes turned to the subject of marriage, but I still found it hard to make out what Hitler's own views on this were. He used to tell the story of one of his old friends, Ernst Hanfstängl, who was usually known as Putzi. For several years this man looked after foreign press affairs, and had been one of the people who had helped Hitler in his early days by introducing him to Munich society. 'Hanfstängl had a very pretty wife and he was unfaithful to her with someone else who wasn't at all nice-looking,' he told us. Clearly, Hitler couldn't understand that a woman's beauty in itself wasn't enough to make a good marriage. On the other hand, it wasn't only Eva Braun's looks that attracted him to her.

He loved to talk about Eva, and it was always affectionately. He telephoned her every day, and whenever an enemy attack on Munich was announced he paced the floor like a caged beast waiting for the attack to be over and the telephone lines re-established so that he could speak to her. Once when Eva's house was damaged Hitler talked of nothing but her courage all day long. 'She never goes down into the bomb shelter, even though I beg her to because one day that place is going to collapse like a house of cards. She won't go to my apartment either, even though she'd be completely safe there. I finally persuaded her to have a shelter built, but she just invites all her neighbours to use it while she goes up on the roof to watch for fire bombs. She's very brave and very proud. When I first knew her she worked for Heinrich Hoffmann, and only got paid a tiny salary which meant she couldn't afford any luxuries at all. It was several years before she'd even let me pay for taxis for her, and for a long time she slept on a sofa in the office so that I could get hold of her on the telephone, since she didn't have one at home. She finally accepted one present: her little house in Bogenhausen, in Munich.'

So from what he said it seemed that Eva's qualities as a person were what he most appreciated about her. One day when we were talking about marriage, I asked him why he had never married. After all, I knew from personal experience how much he liked arranging other people's marriages. His reply was rather surprising: 'I wouldn't have been a good family man and I feel it would have been irresponsible of me to set up a home, since I wouldn't have been able to give enough time to my wife. Besides, I didn't want children. I think the children of a genius often have a very hard time, because they're expected to possess the same gifts as their famous parents and they can't be forgiven for being mediocre. Anyway, it's quite common for them to be mentally deficient.'

It was the first time I'd heard from Hitler's own mouth such proof of his *folie de grandeur*. Until then I had sometimes glimpsed his megalomania, from his fanatical views, but he was usually careful not to let it show when talking of his own position. It was more common to hear him say he was the 'instrument of Fate'. 'I must follow the road on which a Superior Will has placed me.' That day, I was deeply shocked to hear a man in all seriousness proclaim himself a genius.

In the course of these conversations at mealtimes Hitler refrained from talking about anything to do with the war, but it was obvious that he had severe worries. He would launch into long monologues addressed more to himself than to us, and when that happened his face showed signs of the desperate frustration and furious tempers that tormented him during his briefing sessions with his staff. 'You can't conduct a war with incompetent generals,' he used to say. 'I ought to follow Stalin's example: he purged his army pitilessly.' Then he would suddenly remember that the women present were not supposed to understand anything about these matters, and he would throw off his black thoughts and become the attentive host again.

There were sometimes interesting discussions about general subjects, although in fact one couldn't really call them discussions, because the simplest remark or question would start Hitler off on a lengthy dissertation of his views that we were all required to listen to. He would talk about religion, for instance. He had absolutely no time for the Church and considered the Christian faith a hypocritical institution which corrupted men. His religion was the laws of nature, and his violent dogma accorded better with them than with the Christian doctrine of loving one's neighbour and even one's enemy. 'Science hasn't yet established the roots of the human species. The only thing that's certain is that we are the highest stage of development in mammals, having begun as reptiles and ended up as Man, passing through a phase as monkeys on the way perhaps. We're a link in the chain of creation; we're children of nature, and the laws that govern all living creatures apply to us too. Anything that's ill-adapted to life, or not strong enough, gets eliminated. It's only Man himself, and especially the Church, that have decided artificially to prolong the lives of the weak, the misfits and those who are inferior.'

I can only remember a tiny part of all Hitler's theories, and I'm not capable of the power of persuasion with which he expounded them. On the way back to our quarters, I used to force myself to try to remember all he'd said so that I could write it down. But I must admit that, the next day, the things that had so impressed me the previous evening seemed increasingly obscure and hazy when I discussed them with my friends, and I couldn't even reconstitute the arguments exactly. If I had been more mature and experienced at the time, I'd never have let myself be carried along and I wouldn't have accepted Hitler's influence uncritically. I'd have realized the dangerousness of a man who, by the sheer force of his gift of oratory, was able to carry millions with him and bend their will and their beliefs to his own.

Occasionally I used to see some of Hitler's advisers, generals or other close colleagues coming out of a meeting with him, their faces contorted, chomping on their cigars as if chewing over thoughts they couldn't put into words. Later I talked to some of them, and they told me how – although they were so much more experienced than me – they often came to see Hitler armed with foolproof arguments and an unshakeable resolve, ready to explain to the Führer that certain of his orders were impossible to carry out or that a certain attack was impossible to mount. But as soon as they were face to face with him Hitler would launch into a great speech, before they'd even had a chance to put forward their theories, and they found their resolution eroded, their objections seemingly demolished and their facts in doubt. They knew all the time that Hitler's arguments were inaccurate, but he succeeded in confusing them completely. When they left him they'd be filled with doubts about things they'd fervently believed a few minutes earlier. It was as if they were hypnotised. Several of them had tried to break free of the influence, but had given up the struggle. They were outmanoeuvred, and in the end they just let things take their fatal course. But as I've said, I had to go through countless deep disappointments, the débâcle of the regime and the tragic end to it all before I could see it clearly.

Meanwhile, my daily life continued smoothly. I enjoyed the summer in the midst of the forest and beside the lakes. I can barely remember all the terrible events the rest of the world was living through in that year of 1943, when German towns and cities were beginning to feel the weight of the war through the danger from the sky. In one of his great speeches Goering had said: 'If a single enemy aircraft manages to appear in the sky over Berlin, then my name is Meyer!' – in other words, it was impossible. But now the sirens were wailing over the whole of Germany, Berlin included. At the GHQ bunkers and defences were being built or reinforced, and the surrounding forests were being filled with barbed wire and mines.

At about this time a new woman appeared at the Wolfsschanze, introduced by Professor Morell. Her name was Marlene von Exner; she was to be Hitler's dietician, and from then onwards she was to be responsible for cooking for him. She was greeted with interest by the men and with chilly reserve by the other women. It was only after we'd moved into a huge new building, where the rooms were light and comfortable, that I got to know her properly. We became great friends, and I discovered how it was that she'd arrived at the Wolfsschanze.

Marlene von Exner was Viennese, an assistant dietician at the University Clinic in Vienna; out of the blue one day she'd received an invitation to go to Bucharest to treat Marshal Antonescu, who suffered from his stomach and had to follow a strict diet. Her treatment was so successful that her patient was cured in a few months. When the two heads of state with fragile digestive systems, Hitler and Antonescu, met in Salzburg in the spring, they compared notes on their common malady, and as soon as he got back Hitler demanded that his personal physician should find him a dietician like the one who had cured Antonescu. Morell prided himself on the effectiveness of his various injections and mysterious pills, but he couldn't refuse to carry out an order, so he in turn went to the University of Vienna to ask Frau von Exner to come and take charge of the Führer's diet. She wasn't in the least pleased by the offer, since she wanted to continue her own independent career, but in the end she accepted Dr Morell's proposition.

A little older than me, she was twenty-four when she arrived. She had dark hair and a good figure, and possessed all the charm of the Viennese as well as an open and happy nature. Hitler now had a fifth female guest at table. He enjoyed hearing her stories of Vienna and everything she had to say about her family. Her father was a well-known doctor and she had several brothers and sisters; at the time when the National Socialists were struggling in secret in Austria they had been convinced Nazi supporters, and later became party members. But when Hitler's *Gauleiter* imposed the full strictures of the Nazi regime in Vienna and the war spread to Austria, their admiration had lost much of its initial glow. The newcomer left Hitler in no doubt as to the resentment felt by the Viennese: 'Sir, you promised to make Vienna the pearl of Austria, but your people are destroying all the fine things of old Viennese culture and bringing nothing new to replace them. Why do you give so much preference to Linz?'

Hitler accepted her reproaches and remained good-tempered because he was so happy with her culinary talent, delighted by her Austrian cakes and especially pleased with her skill in making his vegetarian soups. He never guessed how unhappy his taste in food made her, though. With Antonescu she'd been able to have caviar and lobster, despite the Marshal's diet, and had also had the opportunity to cook elegant dishes for large dinner parties and receptions. But Hitler still only wanted his eternal carrots, potatoes and fried eggs. 'He can't live long on food like that,' she used to say, and she secretly put marrow bone in his vegetable soup. She smoked like a chimney and I often told her that, if she wanted to be relieved of her duties as cook to the Führer, all that was needed was for him to find a cigarette butt in his morning chocolate.

A little later Antonescu paid a visit to the GHQ, and was delighted to see Marlene again. On his return to Romania he sent her by air a young dog, the offspring of a pair of fox terriers she'd looked after during her stay in Bucharest. He was a tiny little puppy for whom the smallest lump of grass was an insurmountable obstacle, and although he always remained small he was a beautiful little dog and full of character.

But Hitler thought this gift completely unworthy of a head of state, a Marshal to boot, and wasted no time in giving Marlene another dog. 'I can do better than that Balkan,' he boasted, and he ordered Martin Bormann to unearth the most beautiful fox terrier, with the best pedigree available. Marlene von Exner was at her wits' end. 'What am I going to do with two dogs, when I spend the whole day in the kitchen?' she wailed. The dog, whose name was Purzel, didn't take long to arrive, and Hitler offered it to Marlene with great pride: it was a superb animal which had carried off several major prizes at dog shows. It was calm, dignified, a bit stupid and unable to do anything except strike poses and bask in the spectators' admiration.

12

'Panic Will Spread Throughout England!'

On 19 July 1943 Hitler flew to Italy for a meeting with Mussolini, and I went with him. The journey was top secret and even the people who were going didn't know about it until the last moment. The previous evening we had dinner with Hitler, but he didn't mention a word about it. The next morning I noticed an unusual amount of activity around the Führer's bunker: orderlies were going about their duties much earlier than usual; people were carrying suitcases; Schaub was behaving more self-importantly than ever. I thought that a reception of some kind must have been planned at the last minute, but just to be on the safe side I packed a bag with all the office necessities.

Suddenly the telephone rang, and Linge's voice said, 'Have you got a uniform?'

'No, I've never had a uniform.'

'Well, you'll stay at the airport, then' – and before I could ask him what all this was about he hung up.

I rushed off to find Schaub since, in his capacity as chief aide-de-camp, he was supposed to let me know if I was needed. He seemed embarrassed, and burbled a few incomprehensible words before finally telling me I should get myself ready to leave for the airport. To my questions about our destination, he replied that it was top secret. I burst out laughing and went to see Linge, hoping to get some more precise information, but he was too busy to say more than that the trip was due to last three days. Since the situation on the Russian front was very serious, I imagined that Hitler was going to inspect the armies of the Ukraine.

I left for the airport in the company of two stenographers whose job it was to take down the daily briefing sessions word for word. One of them asked me if I knew Italy – and so I finally learnt where we were going.

We took off in four large Condor aircraft, spacious machines with room for about sixteen passengers. I was in the Führer's plane, where he had a seat apart from the rest, just behind the cockpit on the right, with a large table in front of it. All the other seats were arranged as in a restaurant car: in groups of four, each around a small table. The pilot, Hans Baur, gained height with all speed.

We landed close to the Berghof, where we were to spend the night before leaving again at 7.30 the next morning. I'd felt ill during the flight and so went to bed straight after dinner. The next day I got an unpleasant surprise: I'd set my alarm clock early and I was lying in the bath when an orderly called on the telephone to ask what I was doing and to inform me, in a panic-stricken voice, that everyone was waiting for me. I've never dressed so fast in my life. Later, on the plane, I discovered what had happened: the previous evening Hitler had had some doubts about the weather conditions and had decided to bring the flight time forward, but no one had thought to let me know.

We landed somewhere in northern Italy and were then carried in Mussolini's special train to Treviso station, where Hitler, his retinue and all the people who had come to greet him got into cars flanked by carabinieri on motorcycles. The procession set off at a brisk pace towards the meeting place, a sumptuous old villa on the outskirts of the town. I didn't see Hitler or any of his entourage again for the whole day, which I spent sitting in Mussolini's special train, astonished by the dirt and dilapidation of the old carriages and the comic opera uniforms of the staff.

After a sweltering day, the return journey followed the same route, late in the afternoon. This time the flight was very pleasant, with a magnificent sunset over the Alps. We arrived at the Berghof for the night and the next morning returned to the Wolfsschanze.

Hitler's visit to Mussolini turned out to be an evil omen. A few days later the *Duce* was overthrown and became a prisoner in a villa near Rome. Italian Fascism was in a state of collapse. Hitler was beside himself that day, letting out a string of curses, raging at Italy's retreat from the war and bemoaning Mussolini's personal fate. His appalling mood hadn't cleared by the evening, when he was absent-minded and spoke only in monosyllables. Then: 'Mussolini was much weaker than I thought,' he suddenly said. 'I propped him up personally but he fell in spite of it all. In the end we've never been able to count on the Italians as allies and I think we've got a better chance of winning the war alone than with people we can't trust. The Italians have cost us plenty of defeats and losses of prestige, but brought us very few victories.'

I try to force myself to remember all that happened in the days that followed. The time went by, marked by things which seem to me today to have been fatal stages in the course of events which swept everything away, but the whole remains fluid in my memory. Hitler lived as he had done before, working, playing with his dog, screaming at his generals, dining with his secretaries, all the time pushing Europe towards its fate – and we scarcely noticed. Enemy bombs were falling over Germany; the sky was ripped apart by the wail of sirens; on the Eastern Front the fierce fighting had begun again. Yet a few victories and, above all, the irrepressible confidence of the Führer himself, had overlain the darkest days several months earlier when our despair had been at its height. Then, in February 1943, soon after I had started to work for Hitler, Johanna Wolf had come to find me in the bunker, her eyes full of tears. 'We've surrendered at Stalingrad,' she said. 'Our armies are destroyed – dead, or taken prisoner by the Russians!' As she burst into helpless sobbing we both thought of the countless dead, the blood and the suffering. That night Hitler had seemed like an old man, tired and listless: the day had lodged in my memory like a visit to a cemetery.

At the GHQ Hitler devoted some time every evening to having tea with his guests: his secretaries, doctors, aides-de-camp, Ambassador Hewel, the Head of Press, Heinz Lorenz, and the Director of the Chancellery, Martin Bormann. Goering and Himmler never came, but occasionally Albert Speer, Sepp Dietrich and Marlene von Exner put in an appearance. Hitler avoided talking about events at the front. When Speer was there, the conversation took a technical turn: we talked of recent discoveries, new weapons and so on. When Sepp Dietrich came, they aired their memories of the early days of the party, the 'time of combat'. I must say that these evenings were much more interesting at the GHQ than at the Berghof, because the conversation was more intimate – almost confidential – and this helped to keep us awake.

We split the daily duties into two shifts, because it was imposs-

103

ible to go to bed at five or six o'clock every morning and then get up at nine. Hitler was quite understanding: Eva Braun had managed to persuade him that most people needed more sleep, and he didn't like the idea that conversations with him should be seen as a burden. He used to talk about his childhood, about the time when he was a student in Vienna (although in fact he was never properly enrolled in any faculty, since he'd failed the admission examinations to the School of Fine Arts), about his years at the front during the First World War, the struggles in the early days of the Nazi party and the year he spent in prison, at Landsberg, after the failed putsch of November 1923.

But all these stories have slipped my memory, and what remain are the dramatic events I lived through. Yet at the time the effect of these anecdotes was to sustain the image of the Führer as a human being. He considered himself a genius, and was accepted as such by his entourage, and for a long time his successes seemed to provide a justification for this. His memories revealed the private side of his personality: a certain sensitivity and some generous impulses which made it more difficult to spot the dark spirit that haunted this evil genius.

The time I spent close to Hitler, listening to him talk, now seems like an unbroken procession of endless days. Bombs fell; the lines of the battle fronts changed; we attacked Britain with our new weapons, thinking we'd break through to victory. Christmas 1943 arrived, but no one took much notice of it; Hitler ignored it altogether. Not a single branch of holly or ivy, nor a single candle, marked the festival of peace and love. My husband came for a short leave and we spent a brief time together in our chalet, but he had changed a great deal. The man with me was like a stranger; my real husband seemed to have stayed at the front. He couldn't stand the atmosphere back home in Germany, and he was deeply upset when he discovered, through a conversation with the Führer, that Hitler no longer had any clear picture of the situation.

He soon left again for the Russian front, but in the spring of 1944 it was discovered that German prisoners had been forced by means of injections of some sort of truth drug to make statements against their will, so Hitler recalled all the officers who'd been part of his entourage so that what they knew could never be revealed in such a way. My husband was among those brought back and transferred to the Western Front in France.

About this time, Hitler started to speak more and more often

104

about the possibility of a bombing raid on the Wolfsschanze GHQ. 'They know perfectly well where we are,' he'd say, 'and one day they're going to destroy everything in a massive bombardment. I expect them to attack at any moment.' 'They' were the American bombers. There were often alerts, but they were only ever isolated reconnaissance flights over the forests. Our anti-aircraft defences stayed silent, because it was reckoned wiser not to give the reconnaissance planes any indication of the GHQ's whereabouts.

In the spring we went back to the Berghof because the Wolfsschanze installations were to be reinforced. Hitler wanted to build several very secure bunkers, colossal concrete constructions over thirty feet high, and I was horrified at the idea of living like a mole without seeing the light of day. But for the moment the busy life at Obersalzberg began again. Eva Braun was there, fresh and vivacious, with an inexhaustible wardrobe; the guests reappeared, and the war suddenly seemed very far away.

One person was absent from the entourage. Marlene von Exner hadn't come with us, but had stayed at the Wolfsschanze to pack up her kitchen utensils before returning to Vienna. Her fate was tragi-comic. She'd lost her heart to a young SS aide-de-camp called Fritz Darges, even though she couldn't bear Prussians and loathed the SS. But love is blind. The situation was delicate for two reasons: Gretl Braun, Eva's sister, was in love with Darges herself, and there was also something not quite clear about Marlene's background. As soon as she'd entered the Führer's service she'd informed the security officers that her mother's papers were not in order, because her grandmother had been a foundling child and it was impossible to prove her Aryan origins.

Since the family's commitment to National Socialism was devout, Hitler at first didn't pay much attention to the problem. But in the meantime the SD (Security Police), who always worked meticulously on such matters, had discovered that indeed there was some Jewish blood in Marlene's maternal line. Marlene herself was much less worried about the fact that she would lose her job with Hitler than about the impossibility of her marrying a member of the SS. Hitler had an interview with Marlene, in the course of which he said, 'I'm very sorry for you, but you must understand that I have no choice but to remove you from my staff. . . . It's impossible for me to make exceptions to my own rules just because they go against my own interests. As soon as you get back to Vienna I will personally Aryanize your whole family, and I shall continue to pay your salary for the next six months.'

That's how Marlene left us. I was present when Hitler gave Martin Bormann the order to deal with the Aryanization of the Exner family, but it was obvious that the task went against the grain with Bormann. He had made advances to the pretty Viennese girl himself but had been rejected, and he wasn't a man to forgive easily. His vengeance was swift. Several weeks later, I had a very sad letter from Vienna in which Marlene told me that her family had all had their party membership cards withdrawn, and were in trouble. When I asked Bormann about this, he assured me he'd fix it – but some weeks went by and I received a second letter, containing terrible news. Life had become impossible for the whole family: Marlene's sister couldn't get a place in the Faculty of Medicine; her brother had had to abandon his medical practice; and the youngest brother wasn't allowed to go into the army.

I was furious. I sat down in front of the typewriter with the large typeface and typed out the whole letter, which I then showed to Hitler. He flushed red with anger and immediately called Bormann, who in turn was bright red by the time he left the Führer's office. He threw me a look of pure hatred as he passed. But shortly afterwards I got the good news that everything had been fixed, their Aryanization was at last official and Marlene thanked me warmly on behalf of all her family.

That spring at the Berghof life was even more disorganized than ever. The conferences were interminable; meals took place at ridiculous times and Hitler prolonged the evening gatherings more and more. The apparent vivacity, the chattiness and the ever more numerous new guests couldn't, however, chase away the anxiety in everyone's hearts. Hitler's military entourage knew the extent of his worries and the truth about the situation at the fronts, but those of us who didn't, tried to believe in his assurances and in his faith in victory, and to stifle their crippling doubts.

Eva Braun sought me out to ask me how the Führer was. 'I don't want to ask Dr Morell, because I haven't much confidence in him and I can't stand him. But I was horrified when the Führer arrived at the Berghof – he looks much older, and he seems so preoccupied. Do you know what his troubles are? He never talks to me about that kind of thing, but I don't think the situation can be very good. Frau Junge, you know the Führer well and you see him every day: you can guess what's on his mind. The military communiqués must be enough to worry anyone in command.'

During the walks to the tea house, Eva reproached Hitler for walking with a stoop. 'I'm carrying a bundle of keys in my pocket which is much too heavy,' he replied, jokingly, 'and I've got a huge sack of troubles on my shoulders.' He couldn't resist teasing Eva about her taste for elegant clothes. 'Besides, I'm adapting myself to you. You wear high heels to make yourself look taller, I stoop a bit, and then we're better matched.'

'I'm not small,' she protested. 'I'm one metre sixty-three, like Napoleon!'

Nobody knew Napoleon's height, least of all Hitler. 'How do you know Napoleon was one metre sixty-three?'

'It's a well-known fact. Any well-educated person knows that,' Eva replied, but that evening she went straight to the library to consult an encyclopedia. Sadly, there was nothing in it about Napoleon's height.

It snowed incessantly during early 1944. The snow piled up on the terrace and formed towers against the walls. Eva was very keen to go skiing but Hitler wouldn't let her, saying that it was too dangerous and she might break a leg. She had to be content with long walks, and she was often absent at lunchtime. It was still snowing in April, and the snow was lying twenty feet deep a thousand feet up in the mountains.

Then, with the spring, enemy aircraft reappeared over Berchtesgaden. After the invasion of Italy the Allies had captured so many vantage points to the south that the squadrons could easily reach across Austria into Bavaria. Our area was flown over every day, the sirens starting in the early morning when we were just getting the chance to snatch some sleep. The machines installed to spread a layer of artificial fog over the Führer's residence were put into action, and the whole region was wrapped in thick cloud. As at the Wolfsschanze, the Führer expected a massive attack on the Berghof. For months work had been going on to build a vast network of shelters in the Obersalzberg mountain. In several places the rocks had been pierced by machines which dug out long galleries leading to the shelters, but only the large bunker of the Berghof was finished. Opposite the back entrance, near the living room, a wide door led straight into the rocky mountainside. There were sixty-five steps leading down to an air raid shelter which contained everything that Hitler, his numerous colleagues and all his entourage needed for their day-to-day existence.

I had visited the living quarters but never the storage areas for provisions and for the archives which had been brought there. Almost every morning the guests met in the depths of the mountain, half asleep and clutching their suitcases, but despite the sirens there was never an attack. We were directly on the squadrons' line of approach, but the air raids' targets were always Vienna, precise locations in Hungary or the Bavarian towns. Often, when the artificial fog had cleared, we could see the reddish glow of Munich in flames.

Whenever that happened, Eva found it almost impossible to stay put. She pleaded with Hitler to let her to go to Munich in her car to see if her house was still standing. Of course Hitler refused her permission to go, and then Eva would spend hours on the telephone giving instructions or gathering news. But when one of her best friends, the Munich actor Heini Handschuhmacher, was killed in an air raid, nothing could stop her: she left with her friend Herta Schneider and her sister Gretl to attend the funeral. She came back deeply upset, bringing terrible news about the suffering of the town's population. Hitler listened to her account with a grave face, and then swore to take heavy revenge: 'The Luftwaffe's new weapons will make the enemy pay a hundred times over for what they've done to us.'

He was talking of the V1s and V2s, which began to be launched against Britain later in 1944. 'Panic will spread throughout England!' Hitler cried. 'The effect of these weapons on the nerves is unbearable. No one can do anything to resist them. I'm going to take my revenge in the very homes of these barbarians who are dropping their bombs on our women and children and destroying our German culture!'

But the reports he received of the Luftwaffe's anti-aircraft defences were crushing. I remember one daylight bombing raid on Munich. Hitler wanted to know exactly what forces had been deployed in defence, and Colonel von Below spent some time on the telephone getting precise information. In the end he had to give the Führer the answer: 'Six fighters were supposed to take off, but three didn't manage to get into the air, two had to double back because of technical problems, and the sixth, finding himself alone, felt himself powerless to launch the attack.' Hitler went green with fury. Even though he was surrounded by guests, he couldn't restrain himself from exploding with rage against the Luftwaffe and against Goering.

We continued to be roused from our beds on a daily basis and

With Mussolini at the Wolfsschanze. The roof was covered in grass to camouflage it from enemy planes. *(Paris Match)*.

Eva Braun,
General Hermann
Fegelein and his
wife Gretl Braun.
(Copress, Munich).

The night before
the wedding at
Traudl Humps'
house in Munich.

The marriage of
Traudl Humps and
Hans Junge,
performed by a
registrar in
Munich, June 1943.

After the wedding.

With Albert Speer.

With Mussolini and
Field Marshal
Keitel at the
Wolfsschanze.

Relaxing in the
Obersalzburg
mountains.

The map chamber
at the
Wolfsschanze.

Above: Awarding medals to the Hitler Youth, 20 April 1945.

Below: The last official photograph of Hitler, with Artur Axman on the right. *(Keystone Collection).*

Above and below: Berlin was razed to the ground by enemy bombing.

Traudl Junge in Munich, 1986. *(Jan Cook)*.

rushed into our underground hideaways. The ritual was repeated so often, and still not a single bomb fell anywhere near the Berghof, that we gradually lost the urge to leave our beds and take refuge. Even Hitler no longer went down the sixty-five steps into the shelters unless the anti-aircraft flak began, or there was a real attack on targets not far away. Instead he stood by the entrance and watched, like a guard dog, to make sure nobody left the bunker before the end of the alert. Eva Braun was the particular object of his surveillance. One day, after the sirens began, I went down into the gallery to see if everyone was already assembled, but I found no one there at all. I went back up the steps, but just in front of the entrance I saw Hitler standing chatting to Bormann and Hewel. When he saw me he shook his finger at me and said, 'Don't be so rash, young lady, and go straight back down into the shelter. The alert isn't over yet.' Since I didn't want to betray Eva or all the others who hadn't even bothered to get out of bed, I went down again without saying a word. Twice more I tried to leave the bunker, but Hitler was still standing guard at the entrance and it wasn't until the signal for the end of the raid sounded that I could get out.

At mealtimes, Hitler would deliver a speech on the absolute necessity of going down into the bunker the moment the alarms went off. 'It isn't a sign of courage but a sign of stupidity if you don't look after your own safety,' he'd say. 'And since my colleagues are irreplaceable, they have a special duty to get themselves into the bunker. It's ridiculous to imagine you're making a display of bravery by exposing yourself to the danger of getting killed by a bomb.' He wasn't thinking of me, of course, but of the great majority of his officers and other colleagues who didn't believe there was any risk of an attack on the Berghof and who were therefore unwilling to waste hours underground.

During our stay at the Berghof in the spring of 1944, Hitler brought together at the Platterhof the commanders-in-chief of the land army, officers of the General Staff and the commanders of various divisions, so that he could boost their morale. Similarly, the heads of great industrial enterprises and political leaders were summoned to receive instructions from the Führer. Even though Hitler gave long speeches on these occasions I never had to take dictation, because when he was speaking in front of a circle of intimates he never needed a script. The speeches weren't intended to be heard by the public, and he preferred to speak spontaneously and freely.

Among the military high command was Field Marshal Dietl, supreme commander of the Chasseurs Alpins in Norway. He had come straight from the front and Hitler had awarded him the Knight's Cross with diamonds on this occasion. The Führer admired him greatly and held long conversations with him. Naturally enough, Dietl wanted to take the opportunity of paying a brief visit to his wife, but Hitler advised him not to leave until late in the morning because the atmospheric conditions around Salzburg were often very unfavourable. Dietl, however, was impatient to go, and his plane took off at first light in spite of the mist: when Hitler woke up he learnt that the fine Field Marshal, with his brand-new cross set with diamonds, had been the victim of a fatal accident.

Hitler was deeply upset by the news, but at the same time furious with Dietl for having been so irresponsible about his own safety. He repeated his strictures about the duty of his staff not to take pointless risks. A few weeks later there was another plane crash not far from Salzburg, and once again the victim was a high-ranking officer, General Hube. In the same plane was Ambassador Hewel, who was taken to hospital in Salzburg, seriously wounded.

Meanwhile, a new face had appeared in Hitler's entourage. SS Gruppenführer Hermann Fegelein was the liaison officer between Hitler and Himmler and held a post on the Führer's General Staff. At first he only came to the briefing sessions, but once he had made firm friends with Martin Bormann he very quickly became the life and soul of the party at the Berghof. Fegelein was the perfect romantic hero type. He had incredible cheek, and wore the Knight's Cross with swords and oak leaves – so it wasn't surprising that he was used to women falling into his arms. He was also witty, and used to tell funny and often risqué stories without a shadow of embarrassment. He was reputed to be a force of nature, and he believed it himself: he'd risen rapidly, and rather unexpectedly, in his career.

Fegelein never missed one of Bormann's nocturnal drinking sessions, drinking to *Brüderschaft* (brotherhood) with all the important people. This involved proposing a toast, then drinking with linked arms, and it signified very close friendship. All the women threw themselves at him. Anyone who wasn't his friend was his enemy, as soon as he felt his position was safe enough. He was cunning and had no scruples, but one or two of his character traits were more sympathetic. Among these was the honesty to admit that he was basically very cowardly, and that he owed his decorations to a lucky fluke which had merely looked heroic. In fact, he had been terrified. He also admitted quite openly that nothing mattered to him except his career and a life of pleasure.

Soon after he arrived, frictions and intrigues sprang up in Hitler's immediate entourage. Brilliant talker that he was, Fegelein caught the eye of Eva Braun and her sister Gretl, and the latter became the object of the handsome Hermann's attentions. Before he knew she was Eva's sister, he'd called her a stupid goose; but he changed his mind the moment he discovered her family links. And, before long, we had a great surprise: in April 1944 Hermann and Gretl announced their engagement, and Fegelein's excellent position was doubly secure.

Until then the only person who had a good personal relationship with Hitler was Ambassador Hewel, and Fegelein saw this as an obstacle. He took advantage of Hewel's long absence in hospital in Salzburg to blacken his reputation with the Führer, and, since Hewel was in no position to defend himself, Fegelein succeeded. Hewel fell into disgrace, and when he himself got married Hitler didn't even ask him to introduce his wife.

13

The July Plot

All these little quarrels and petty jealousies quickly lost their importance when on 6 June we heard the news of the Allied landings on the Western Front. Suddenly it had come, the invasion we'd expected for so long, and which we'd always been sure was doomed to failure. My husband, who had been spending a few days' leave at Berchtesgaden, had to rejoin his unit in France without delay.

After the Allied landing, the daily conferences began to last for hours and hours. When they were finally over, we used to study Hitler's face: his expression was grave and worried, his features pinched. His hope of seeing the enemy suffer a clear defeat in the west was a long way from coming true.

At the Berghof, bathed in the early summer sunlight, a half-unreal peace reigned. We went on chatting, laughing, eating and drinking, yet day after day we were invaded by an insidious tension. The distraught face of Julius Schaub got longer and longer, for the very good reason that he was responsible for compiling a report on every air raid, day and night. News of the terrible destruction of towns all over Germany accumulated, and the raids became so numerous that we had to type the reports for the Führer in abbreviated telegraphese. At every briefing session, Goering and his Luftwaffe officers were showered with curses by Hitler. Each *Gauleiter* sent photographs by the hundred of their flattened towns. Hitler looked at the pictures, beside himself with fury – but he never once paid a visit to any of the towns that had suffered.

On my return from a short visit to my mother in Munich, which had just undergone a particularly devastating bombardment, I said to him: '*Mein Führer*, all these photos people show you are a long way from the reality. You should see the poor people in tears, at the end of their tether, standing in front of their burning houses watching everything they have in the world going up in smoke.'

'I know. I know what it's like,' he replied. 'But it's all going to change. We've got new planes, and there'll be an end to this horror very soon.'

Hitler never had a real picture of the country's distress. He never saw the extent of the ruins and the misery of the German people. He just went on talking about future reprisals, merciless revenge and ultimate victory.

As for me, I knew no better and I still believed he must be keeping in reserve some miracle weapon which would save the German people. Like thousands of my generation, I'd been brought up to believe in Hitler's infallibility.

Hitler was now impatient to get back to the Wolfsschanze, to be close to the Russian front. But the new bunkers weren't ready yet, and his staff tried to persuade him to stay at Berchtesgaden. They thought the Führer shouldn't go too far from the Western Front, where the fierce fighting was taking place. But the situation in the east was just as bad.

As our stay at Berchtesgaden was prolonged, summer weather set in. The peaks of the mountains were still capped with snow, but we could bathe in the Königsee and the surrounding lakes. Life would have been sweet, had we not had the sensation of sitting on a powder keg. More and more, we all strove to hide our fears. Among his intimates Hitler made a show of his certainty of victory, as ever, but wasn't it just a façade? He tried to relax, chatted with the women and changed none of his habits: the walks to the tea house, the long evenings around the fire. People talked about the past and listened to music. Sometimes, none the less, the Führer seemed far away, his gaze absent, and he suddenly looked old and overcome by fatigue. Although he'd always been such a charmer when ladies were present, he no longer worried about what he looked like and didn't hesitate to ask our permission to put his feet up, or even to stretch out on the sofa; at those times Eva's eyes showed her deep distress and anxiety. She was more attentive than ever, more welcoming than ever towards Hitler's guests, and she no longer absented herself from meals or from the evenings by the fire, as was her habit when she found the company not to her liking.

In July Hitler decided he wasn't going to wait any longer, and he left the Berghof for the Wolfsschanze. His new bunker wasn't yet ready, but it didn't matter. He declared that he'd live in the bunker for the aides-de-camp and guests. We were on the way to East Prussia early in the month.

The building work at the GHQ had changed it completely and I could hardly recognize it. Instead of the numerous bunkers, all that was now visible were enormous structures of concrete and steel sticking up between the trees. Yet from the air nothing could be seen but the forest, because a layer of grass had been laid on the roofs of these huge constructions, as well as trees and bushes growing artificially in wooden tubs. The living quarters were much smaller and the furnishings more modest. For his daily conferences Hitler had chosen a nearby chalet which had actually been intended for guests and which contained a large living room, where long tables for the maps of the General Staff had been placed.

We four secretaries were together again. It was full summer by now, and very hot, with not a single cloud in the deep blue sky. We could hardly breathe in the camp huts and we preferred to work in the bunkers, where it was much cooler. Mosquitoes and flies made life outside almost unbearable. The soldiers on guard wore gauze masks to protect their faces, and there were mosquito nets at all the windows. Hitler loathed the weather. He no longer went out with Blondi, whom he entrusted to Sergeant Major Tornow, the official in charge of looking after the dogs. He was perpetually in a bad mood, and complained of migraines and insomnia; his need for relaxation became ever more pressing.

As the situation worsened every day, we spoke less and less about the war. Our only news from the various theatres of operations came from the daily communiqué of the High Command which was pinned on a board at the entrance to the mess, next to the day's menu and the films to be shown.

July 20 1944 was a turning-point in Hitler's fate. That morning, after breakfast, I wrote a long letter to a friend and then went to join my colleague Gerda Christian. We got on our bicycles and went off to swim in a little lake in the restricted zone, something we often did in hot weather. We came back to the GHQ before midday, in case the Führer needed us, since Gerda and I were on duty that day. Johanna Wolf and Christa Schroeder were sleeping, as they'd been on duty the night before.

As we passed the bunker and the adjoining chalet, we realized that the conference was still in progress. The cars were still parked

next to the camp huts. Everything was quiet. We'd got backto
our respective rooms and I was starting to write a letter to my
husband when I heard an enormous explosion. It didn't surprise
me too much, because from time to time a deer used to set
off one of the defensive mines in the surrounding forest, and
occasionally new weaponry was tested nearby. But soon afterwards I heard a hysterical voice shouting for a doctor. I ran
straight out of my room towards the spot where the noise was
coming from, taking a small path through the trees leading to
the bunker. Just before I got there I almost ran into General Jodl
and General Walzenecker, their clothes torn and bloody. The
other secretaries had come running too, but we were stopped
from going any closer.

By then we understood that something very serious had
happened, and Otto Günsche gave us a quick explanation.
'There's been a bomb,' he said, 'but don't worry. The Führer
isn't hurt. You'll see him soon. He's already back in his bunker.'
We went to find the Führer, who was standing in the antechamber
with Martin Bormann at his side. He looked strange. His hair
was standing up on end, and he looked like a hedgehog. His
trousers were in rags. Yet in spite of it all he was euphoric: he
had survived, hadn't he? He said, 'Once again, Providence has
saved me. That proves I'm on the right track. I feel confirmed in
my mission.'

As for the assassination attempt itself, it was thought that
workmen carrying out building work must have been responsible:
one of them could have brought in the explosive and placed it
under the floor of the chalet. Hitler told us yet again that he'd
been saved by Providence, because if he'd given orders that the
conference was to take place in the bunker he would now be
dead. An explosion in the bunker would have brought hundreds
of tons of concrete crashing down, whereas in the chalet, which
was above ground and only made of wood, people were on the
whole injured rather than crushed to death. People have often
said that the meeting was held in the chalet that day, unusually,
to save time because Mussolini – who had been sprung from
captivity – was expected early in the afternoon. In fact, it was
held in the chalet quite regularly.

Very soon after the explosion we met one of Hitler's orderlies,
a small young officer called Mandl, who was full of pride at
having witnessed the momentous events. He told us in detail
what had happened. He was present when Hitler, expounding his

theories about the perpetrators of the attempt, said: 'Stauffenberg was lucky. He was the only one who wasn't at the meeting.' That remark made everyone think about the moment when Stauffenberg had left the room, claiming he had to make a very urgent telephone call. Someone was sent to ask the switchboard operator if he'd seen Colonel Claus von Stauffenberg. 'I saw him come past, but he didn't make a phone call and he left immediately.' His words aroused completely new suspicions: until that point everybody, including Hitler, had been convinced that some of the workmen must have been responsible.

In the hours following the bomb, there was utter confusion in the camp. Orders and counter-orders flew in all directions; the GHQ had become hell. Nobody could be sure who might or might not have been part of the plot. We'd discovered that, after he'd left the conference room, Colonel von Stauffenberg had hurried to the switchboard, then to the office of General Erich Fellgiebel, the officer in charge of telecommunications, and had waited there until the bomb went off. Immediately afterwards he jumped into his Volkswagen and drove to the landing strip. As he passed he must have seen the chalet completely destroyed and apparently lifeless bodies scattered on the ground, and he must have assumed that the assassination attempt had succeeded.

We knew very little about events in Berlin, apart from the fact that Major Remer, commander of the Grossdeutschland regiment, had taken charge of the situation. He'd gone to Goebbels, who'd ordered him to place his troops around the Chancellery buildings and the radio station to prevent the conspirators from taking control of them. He was given the Knight's Cross by the Führer himself for his action.

In the evening, when I saw Hitler again, he was still foaming with rage and indignation. 'These conspirators are traitors, cowards and imbeciles,' he screamed. 'If they'd tried to shoot me, I'd have had a bit of respect for them, at least. But no – they wanted to save their own skins. It's incredible that they think they could do better than me in the position we're in. Those numbskulls have no idea of the chaos there'd be in the whole of Germany if I let go of the reins of power. But I'll make an example of them – an example to anyone else who wants to try the same thing.'

His eyes flashed sparks. He had recovered all his old energy. His only injury was to one shoulder, dislocated by the heavy table top which had flown into the air and crashed down on him.

Almost all the officers who had been present had burst eardrums, multiple injuries or concussion of a more or less serious sort. Four of them had been killed outright, and a fifth, General Schmundt, died two days later. But Hitler didn't even interrupt the day's programme. Dr Morell gave him some mysterious injections, then he went off to welcome Mussolini, who was due to arrive at three o'clock.

Gerda Christian and I were on duty that evening, and Hitler was particularly dynamic. He was like quicksilver. It was clear that the day's adventure had given him a new sparkle and enthusiasm: escaping death so unexpectedly had a miraculous effect on him. It was as if he was high on a drug. Mussolini stayed for a couple of hours, and before he left Hitler showed him the ruins of the chalet and said: 'You see, it was flattened. And I came out without a scratch.'

Later I felt that the assassination attempt of 20 July was the greatest misfortune which could have happened to Germany and to Europe, not because it took place but because it failed. All the unlucky flukes that had prevented the plot from succeeding were interpreted by Hitler as proof of the protection of Providence, and his blind confidence, his certainty of victory, his feeling of omnipotence, his *folie de grandeur* then went beyond all reasonable limits. And if the recent military defeats his armies had suffered might have led him to seek a compromise – deep down, he had begun to doubt his chances of eventual victory – he was once again as certain as ever of his supernatural power. He would fight on to ultimate victory!

That same evening, Hitler decided to address the German people. A mobile radio station arrived from Königsberg to record the speech. A little before midnight, we were all assembled around the Führer in the tea house. The officers whose injuries were not too serious were there as well: General Jodl with a bandage on his head, Marshal Keitel with his hands dressed, and others whose faces were covered in strips of sticking plaster. They looked like men returned from a battlefield.

Hitler delivered a brief speech whose purpose was to reassure the German people that he was invulnerable. He thanked Destiny for having protected Germany from a great tragedy; he urged the people to keep up their faith in victory and to pit all their strength to that end. I was distraught, but it never occurred to me that all over the country millions of people were listening to those words and cursing the trick of fate that had saved Hitler.

When the speech was over we went back to the bunker, and Hitler called Dr Morell to examine him. His pulse was normal, and Hitler was proud of the fact. He needed to be convinced of his invulnerability just once more.

14

Widowed at Twenty-Four

After the attempt on his life, Hitler made no change in his daily habits or his nocturnal monologues over a cup of tea. He even began to invite guests who weren't part of his usual circle. 'I've had enough of soldiers,' he said. The aides-de-camp racked their brains to find dinner guests capable of amusing the Führer. Heinrich Hoffmann was always a last resort but alcohol had made him practically senile, even though he was only fifty-nine, and Hitler no longer appreciated his company very much. On the other hand Professor Giesler, an architect and builder, proved more the type of guest that Hitler wanted. A creative man and a real artist, he was none the less a talented clown who could perform skilful impersonations of members of the Führer's entourage. He was especially funny when imitating Robert Ley, the director of the Reich's political organization and the Labour Front – his way of speaking and walking, his gestures. Ley had a speech defect which made him pronounce every word very slowly, and most of the time he made such silly remarks that it was difficult to take him seriously.

One day, while making a speech, Ley had cried out to the assembled audience: 'I have become more beautiful and Germany is overjoyed!' – he had intended to say the opposite: 'Germany has become more beautiful and I am overjoyed!' Giesler made Hitler roar with laughter by repeating gaffes of this sort made by Ley, but at the same time the Führer felt a certain embarrassment about this ridicule of one of his close colleagues, someone who occupied one of the highest posts in the regime's hierarchy. He probably realized that the element of comedy wouldn't be lost on a great many Germans. So after having a good laugh at Ley's expense Hitler always felt obliged to say, 'Ley is an old and faithful party comrade, an idealist, and he has succeeded in building a faultless organization. I can always count on him.' Hitler showed the same tolerance to other party veterans, but was merciless towards quite reasonable people who had the courage to contradict him or to express any reservations whatsoever.

Another guest who sometimes appeared at the GHQ was Professor Bernd von Arend, a painter and model-maker at the Reichsnationaltheater. His official title was *Reichsbüh–enbildner*, and all such titles now seem ridiculous to me. We mocked them at the time by calling the sergeant who looked after the dogs the *Reichshundführer* (Imperial Dog-walker), Dr Theo Morell *Reichsspritzenmeister* (Imperial Master of Injections), and Heinrich Hoffmann *Reichstrunkenheld* (Imperial Drinking Champion). Of course a theatrical model-maker, however imperial, had no real place at a military GHQ, especially in wartime. But he was there to amuse the Supreme Military Commander, and that probably served some useful purpose. I should add that people from the theatre world had no uniform in the Third Reich hierarchy, but secretly the most eminent artistes had been given a rank and could if necessary parade themselves dressed in the 'uniform of honour' of National Socialism.

For a long time to come, the failed assassination attempt of 20 July was still the principal subject of most of our conversations. A shocked Eva Braun had written a distraught letter which had touched the Führer so deeply that he sent her his tattered trousers as a keepsake.

Despite his supposed invulnerability, the Führer had to consult a specialist from Berlin about the violent headaches he was suffering, which Professor Morell's injections did nothing to alleviate. At the Wolfsschanze he went out very little and ate almost nothing. His left hand had begun to shake. He joked about it, saying, 'Before the attempt on my life, it was my right leg that trembled. Now it's my left hand. Luckily, it stopped on the way and didn't reach my head – what would I look like with my head wobbling all the time?'

At long last a new subject of conversation emerged to fill the evenings at the fireside: Blondi was to start a family and Hitler was looking for a partner worthy of her. He decided upon the German shepherd owned by Gerdy Troost, the architect's widow, and summoned them to GHQ. But Blondi, far from revelling in the company of such a handsome male, paid no attention to him at all until his first tentative approach to her, when she bit him hard. Hitler was very disappointed, but wouldn't give up hope. 'They'll get to know each other after a while,' he said, 'and to like each other better. One of these days I'll have a litter of puppies to look after.'

That evening, Frau Troost had tea with us all and the Führer. She continually tried to persuade him to take a few walks. 'This is no life, sir,' she said. 'You never get any fresh air. You might as well paint a forest on the walls of your bedroom and never leave the bunker again!' He laughed, and declared that the climate in East Prussia was so unhealthy that he'd rather stay indoors. Then Frau Troost advised him to have massages. But Hitler had a horror of any physical contact and the very word 'massage' upset him. 'In Munich in 1923, during the putsch, I broke my shoulder. A sergeant major tried to massage it for me but he did me much more harm than good,' Hitler claimed.

After a few days Frau Troost went home, but left behind her dog, Harras. Since he was rejected by Blondi, he started to display a lively interest in a little fox terrier bitch which I had acquired earlier in 1944. His state of perpetual excitement proved too much for him, however, and he began to pine and waste away, but in the end Blondi proved more amenable and one morning a radiant Hitler was able to announce to us all that the two had mated.

Terrible battles were being waged on every front. In the east, the few victories announced by the Wehrmacht communiqués were only defensive successes, and the Russians continued to advance inexorably. In the west, the invasion had grown and put our forces on the defensive. The division in which my husband was serving was involved in bloody battles near Caen, after which it had to double back to be re-equipped with new tanks. On that occasion, my husband was sent on a special mission to the Führer's GHQ. I was getting ready to leave for Munich, because our house had been destroyed in a bombing raid and I wanted to comfort my mother. I met up with my husband in Berlin, and we spent a few days together in the ruins of the city – then I went on to Bavaria and he rejoined his unit in France.

Munich was a picture of desolation. At home everything had been destroyed. There was despair all round: few people still believed in the possibility of victory. I tried to encourage them, but did I really believe in it myself? I mechanically repeated Hitler's words, but I lacked his powers of persuasion; besides, I was overwhelmed by uncomfortable doubts.

Towards the middle of August, Hitler awarded decorations to some of the people who had been wounded in the attempt on his life. Several others had died of their wounds in the meantime. More importantly, he summoned all the highest echelons of the army to hear him deliver a speech which he considered exceptionally important. I wasn't present at this summit meeting, naturally, but I watched the tense, crimson faces of the generals as they left the room in their gleaming uniforms. They were still arguing vociferously in the mess. The Führer had apparently expressed his indignation about the assassination attempt of 20 July in the strongest terms. He'd decided that the 'German salute' – the Nazi salute, in fact – should be obligatory throughout the Wehrmacht. He had also addressed a solemn appeal for the utmost loyalty and discipline to all officers. Some time later, the transcript of this extraordinary meeting passed under my eyes. I had no right to read it, but I glanced quickly at a few pages, and one sentence stuck in my mind: '. . . I thought that at my final hour my officers would all be gathered around me in serried ranks, their swords drawn, in unshakeable fidelity until death itself. . . .' General von Manstein, later Field Marshal, shouted: 'It shall be so, *mein Führer!*' and the text mentioned, in parentheses, that there was frenetic applause. Who could still have thought that Hitler's end would be like that?

At the end of August I went back to the Wolfsschanze. I couldn't stop myself from nagging everyone in the entourage – officers, aides-de-camp, anyone who was supposed to be in the know – with questions: 'Tell me honestly – do you still believe we'll win the war?'

The answers were always the same: 'It's going badly, very badly, but it's not hopeless. We just have to hold on, whatever it costs, until the new weapons are ready to be put into action.'

Every evening Hitler outlined to us his plans for the reconstruction of our great cities. He spoke of them with such passion. When Giesler was present he'd argue about the rebuilding of Germany and Austria down to the smallest details. These plans for Hamburg, Cologne, Munich, Berlin and Linz didn't just exist in Hitler's galloping imagination – they'd taken shape on paper. Sometimes, as we listened in dismay, he'd set out before us these images of the most beautiful cities in the world, with the widest avenues and the highest towers. Everything was going to be much more beautiful than before. He was almost at the point of telling us not to regret the ruin and destruction the country had suffered.

But did he really believe these fine speeches of his? II often wondered at the time, and now I think that he sometimes managed to delude himself into believing it all, using these visions of the future to combat the pessimism that threatened to over-whelm him. It was well in keeping with his cyclothymic nature – Hitler was a manic depressive.

It was now more than a year and a half since I'd left my family, my friends, my own environment and my normal life. Hitler was still very kind to me, and always treated me almost as if I were a child. He liked joking with me. I had to do impersonations for him of a well-known Viennese actor, talk in Saxon dialect and listen to his anecdotes – always the same ones – with delighted attention. But I felt like a prisoner and I was filled with a certain malaise. I would have much preferred to be among modest, simple people, in the milieu to which I belonged but I was not brave enough to leave.

Hitler now took more and more medicine. At each meal his valet handed him at least five different tablets, some to stimulate his appetite, others to ease his digestion, others still to assuage the distending of the stomach he suffered from. And every day Dr Morell came to administer his mysterious injections. Morell himself had been trying to stick to a diet, to lose weight, but his ferocious appetite got the better of him all the time. Hitler was always indulgent towards Morell, as if to a child: when he spoke of him there was both gratitude and compassion in his eyes. He had boundless faith in him.

'Without Morell,' he'd say, 'I couldn't work. He's always been the only person who can keep me going.' In fact no one really knew what it was Hitler suffered from, and no one had been able to establish a precise diagnosis.

During lunch one day at the end of August I had the impression that Hitler was looking at me strangely, in a way that was almost unfriendly. He didn't speak to me once throughout the meal, and when I happened to catch his eye he turned away. I was puzzled, and I wondered whether one of my older colleagues had been telling tales about me. My youth irritated them sometimes. In the end I decided he was simply in a bad mood that day and, since I was the youngest secretary, he was taking it out on me. But a short time later I got a telephone call from General Fegelein. 'Can I come and have a cup of coffee with you?' he asked. I was astonished by this sudden and unexpected request, but none the less I agreed, even though coffee time had long passed.

After quite a while he still hadn't arrived, and the telephone rang again. Fegelein was sorry: the conference had lasted longer than usual, and he asked me to come over. Since I had to walk my dog, it was easy enough to make a detour via his chalet.

'It's nice of you to come,' he said as he opened the door. 'Would you like a glass of schnapps?'

Where is this leading? I wondered. Aloud I said, 'No, thank you. . . . Why have you suddenly decided to invite me to your chalet – you know I'm faithful to my husband. . . .'

Just then he turned towards me, put his hands on my shoulders and said, 'I'd rather say this straight. Your husband has been killed. The Führer has known about it since yesterday but he wanted to have the news confirmed, and he didn't want to tell you himself. If you have any problems or need anything, come and see me – I'll always do my best to help you.' With those words he took his hands off my shoulders and gave me some schnapps. I drank it down in one gulp and dropped into a chair. In the first shock of the news I was incapable of a single thought, and anyway Fegelein gave me no time to think. He started talking and talking, in a voice that seemed to come from a long way away, about this war, the Bolsheviks, everything, everything was rotten. . . . 'One day,' he said, 'things will be better. . . .'

Somehow I found myself outside again, in the open air. A warm summer rain was falling, freshening the atmosphere. I set off along the main road out of the camp and found myself in the middle of bright green fields, with nothing but calm and silence around me. I felt lonelier than ever and terribly sad.

Much later, I returned to my room. I didn't want to see or speak to anyone: I certainly didn't want condolences, or pity. The telephone rang. An orderly asked me if I would be at dinner that evening. 'No,' I said, 'not this evening.' A few minutes later the telephone rang again. This time it was Linge, Hitler's valet. 'The Führer would like to see you, to talk to you, even if you don't stay for dinner. Come straight away.'

All in all, I told myself, the sooner the better.

I was shown into a little room which was the sitting room of Christa Schroeder's apartment, but which the Führer was temporarily using as an office. He came towards me without saying a word, took both my hands and looked into my eyes. 'My dear, this makes me very sad. Your husband was an extraordinary man.' His voice was soft and sad. 'You'll stay with me, won't you? Don't worry about anything, I'll always look after you.' Suddenly everybody wanted to look after me, when my only wish was to be as far away from there as possible.

Not many days afterwards I went back to my usual place at the Führer's table. He felt very ill and it was almost impossible to get him to take part in the conversation. Even Albert Speer, whom he liked so much, couldn't arouse a spark of interest. Hitler just didn't listen. 'I have so many worries,' he used to say sometimes. 'You can't imagine how hard it is to have to find solutions and take decisions all the time. I'm here with you, but I'm completely alone. Nobody can share the burden of my responsibilities.' He repeated these sentences incessantly every time we asked him how he was. Doctors came and went from the bunker. An ear, nose and throat specialist arrived from Berlin, as well as Professor Brandt, who examined Hitler at length to try to determine the cause of his shaking left arm.

Eventually Professor von Eicken, in whom the Führer had great confidence, was called in from Berlin. Professor Morell was himself ill, confined to his bed, and had to concede his place to a Dr Weber. This was terribly hard for the ambitious Morell, since Hitler found that he was very happy under Dr Weber's care and realised that other doctors were also competent to give him injections. Until then Hitler had maintained that it took great skill to find his veins and that only Morell could manage it successfully.

Morell was extremely sensitive and jealous of his position, and could also be vindictive. And now, just at the moment when his Führer had most need of his medical services, he was forced to let himself be replaced. Another danger threatened, too: Dr Brandt and one of his colleagues, Dr von Hasselbach, had established that the tablets Morell prescribed for the Führer contained enough strychnine to have fatal consequences if the Führer went on taking them in massive doses. Besides, nobody checked what medicaments Hitler took during the day: Linge, the valet, had a supply in his medicine cupboard, and whenever Hitler asked for a tablet he gave him one without any reference to Dr Morell.

The two doctors, von Eicken and Brandt, eventually formulated a joint diagnosis which they presented to the Führer. It threw him into a terrible rage. Brandt was immediately stripped of his functions as Hitler's private doctor and forfeited his confidence, even though feelings of friendship still bound him to Hitler and Eva Braun. But anyone who crossed Morell was storing up trouble for the future.

A few days later we were informed that from then on the Führer would take his meals alone. He would no longer put in an appearance at teatime. In fact he'd stay in his room, lying down. This was a great surprise to everyone, since none of us had ever seen Hitler in bed – even his valets woke him in the mornings by knocking on the door of his room and leaving his breakfast tray on a small table in the antechamber. He'd never received anyone, even one of his closest associates, in his dressing gown. And now, suddenly, he was ill. Nobody knew what the matter was. Was it as a result of the attempt on his life? The doctors seemed inclined to think that maybe delayed effects of concussion were making themselves felt.

We didn't see the Führer at all for several days. The orderlies were dismayed because he wouldn't see anyone. Otto Günsche said to me, 'The Führer is completely apathetic. We don't know what to do. He isn't even interested in the situation on the Eastern Front, despite the fact that it's so worrying.' Morell, who was feeling better himself by now, gave his assistants instructions for the Führer's care. And then one day, quite unexpectedly, Hitler rallied, began to issue orders over the telephone, asked for reports from the front and – still without leaving his bed – reinstituted his nocturnal tea-drinking habits.

Hitler's bunker bedroom, where he summoned us all to tea, was sombrely furnished, more like a prisoner's cell than the room of a Supreme Commander. Since there was an enormous wooden kennel for Blondi, there was very little space to move about or simply to relax in. I thought of Eva Braun, who never knew what to give the Führer for Christmas or birthday presents. He wore a thick grey wool dressing gown, a cravat and a pair of very ordinary black shoes – the kind of shoes a simple soldier might have worn. Choosing a present shouldn't have been difficult. He never wore pyjamas, but instead a long white shirt which looked as if it might have been issued by the Wehrmacht. He couldn't button the cuffs because they were too tight, and we could see the sickly white skin of his arms. I understood why he never wore *Lederhosen*, still less a bathing suit.

There weren't many of us around his bed: one or two secretaries, his aide-de-camp Albert Bormann and Ambassador Hewel. When a rare visitor arrived, one of us had to get up to offer them a seat. Hitler spoke very little, preferring to listen to us telling him what we'd been doing for the last few days – despite the fact that the account was bound to be both monotonous and depressing, since our main activity at the time was typing out quantities of reports from all over Germany giving the miserable tally of the ever-increasing bombing raids.

It was both dramatic and pitiful to find oneself face to face with a man who could probably have put an end to this carnage with a stroke of the pen. There he lay, prostrate in bed, almost inert, with dull, staring eyes, while hell raged around him. It was as if his body had suddenly realised the futility of the efforts his brain was making, and refused to comply. Never before had Hitler been in such a state: his body had rebelled against his spirit, and he had succumbed to the first manifestation of physical weakness he'd known.

15

'I Must Win Some Victories'

Meanwhile, the construction work on the new bunker in the Wolfsschanze had come to an end. It was a fortress. Hitler eventually overcame his physical crisis and moved into the colossal subterranean structure with its long passages, large meeting rooms and living quarters. There was a special kitchen to meet the Führer's dietary requirements, and all of his close colleagues had their own rooms. Hitler believed that a huge air raid was possible any day, and he wanted to have his world around him. The other bunkers had been reinforced, too. The air alerts were now a daily occurrence, and Hitler took these reconnaissance flights very seriously, seeing them as warning signals of a large-scale attack.

To the west the Allies were moving towards Germany's borders, and before long the Soviet troops would be in a position to chase us out of East Prussia. On clear autumn days we could hear the gunfire. Hitler had his mind set on ordering new defence works and reinforcements at the GHQ: throughout the forest barricades, pillboxes, minefields, mounds of barbed wire and observation posts sprang up. Paths along which I'd walked my dog the previous day were forbidden territory the next, and we had to show our passes at increasingly numerous control posts. If the enemy had known how much havoc was caused by the smallest air-raid alert, they would certainly have attacked. But miraculously they still did not seem to know the exact whereabouts of the GHQ, because we never suffered a direct attack. It was difficult to get to the air raid shelters in the blackout at night – we kept stumbling into trees and it was almost impossible to get our bearings. We also had to remember the password, since the sentries weren't in a mood for jokes. But with a few exceptions nobody took all this very seriously, because during the day all we had to do was carry our passes, and at night we avoided leaving the inner circle of the camp.

Hitler was trying to create new divisions to send to the front, and as the front shortened he decided to move to his western HQ, in the Taunus mountains, to raise the morale of the troops outflanked by the Allies after the invasion. Early in November 1944 we left the Wolfsschanze, taking all our possessions with us, for the Russians were very close.

Climbing into the special train that would take us from the Wolfsschanze to Berlin that November morning gave me a sad feeling of final separation. I'd got used to life in the forest I loved, and I'd become very attached to the East Prussian landscape. Now we were leaving for ever. Hitler knew it himself, even though he had given orders for new building work just as if he intended to be back soon. Outwardly his mood seemed calm and detached, but that departure couldn't have left him unmoved. Hadn't he always declared that as long as he could hold a piece of the front, he'd never let it go? He had the firm conviction that his personality and willpower were strong enough to achieve the impossible.

The special train was full. Part of the GHQ staff had left an hour earlier. Hitler had calculated the time of the train journey so that we would reach Berlin at dusk and keep his arrival secret. The sun appeared timidly through the mist and rewarded us with a clear late autumn day, but the windows of Hitler's carriage were blacked out and he sat in his compartment in electric light. The midday meal in his carriage was made even gloomier by the fact that we were plunged in tomb-like half-dark while the sun shone brightly outside. Dr Morell, Bormann, Hewel and Schaub were present; Christa Schroeder and Frau Christian were already in Berlin, so Johanna Wolf and I were the only women at the table. I had never seen Hitler so downcast. His voice was scarcely louder than a whisper and his gaze was fixed firmly on his plate or on a corner of the white tablecloth. The narrow 'moving cage' in which we were gathered had an oppressive atmosphere of indefinable anguish.

Abruptly, Hitler began to talk about an operation. I didn't understand what he meant at first, but he was talking about Professor von Eicken and his great faith in him. 'It's a grave responsibility,' Hitler said, 'and he's the only person who could do it. An operation on the vocal chords doesn't carry any fatal risks, but I could lose my voice . . .' Hitler didn't finish his sentence. The operation he needed, to remove a polyp from his vocal chords, was a minor one, but Hitler knew that his voice was the instrument of his power and that his words kept the people in thrall and carried them with him. How could he keep the masses behind him if something went wrong and he couldn't make any more speeches?

In fact, his advisers had been trying for weeks to persuade him to make another speech. '*Mein Führer*, you must address the German people. They're demoralised and beginning to doubt you. There are rumours that you're no longer alive. . . .' The aides-de-camp were even getting the secretaries to ask the Führer whether he wanted to dictate anything. His reply was always the same: 'This isn't the moment to speak. I have to find solutions and act on them. I have nothing to say to the German people just now. I must win some victories first – that's how I'll give people back their strength and courage.'

At that time, a few months after escaping the attempt on his life, another sword of Damocles was hanging over Hitler's head. There were serious problems on every front; he needed to be in the east and the west simultaneously. He chose to stay in Berlin.

We arrived in the evening without raising any alarms, but we had to stop at the Grunewald station because the Silesian station had been destroyed the previous day. By the time we left the guest compartments, Hitler had already disappeared and we could see the red tail-lights of his line of cars moving away. The town was even darker and gloomier than the forest we'd come from. The Führer's car and those of his entourage chose a route through the least damaged streets, so that once again he didn't see the extent of destruction in the capital, even though the cars' dimmed headlights swept a narrow path of light across piles of rubble on either side of the streets.

When we got to the Chancellery a group of people was already waiting in the Ladies' Chamber. This was a vast hall with a huge fireplace, tall mirrors and elegant furniture. It took its name from the now distant days when Hitler gave glittering receptions for artists and theatre people, but by 1944 the heavy carpets had been moved into the bunker and the fine furniture had been replaced by tables and chairs which were quite ordinary but actually more comfortable. Hitler only stayed a short time. We'd had dinner on the train, and he ordered Linge to prepare his bedroom and take Blondi for a walk so that he could retire almost immediately. He was visibly extremely nervous, since his operation was scheduled for the following morning.

Until then I had never spent much time in Berlin with Hitler and his General Staff. It was the first time since the war began that the military GHQ had been transferred to the heart of Germany. The gigantic complex of the Chancellery, bordered by the old streets – Hermann-Goeringstrasse, Voss-strasse and Wilhelmstrasse – still seemed a frightening labyrinth to me. I knew Hitler's former residence in the ancient Wilhelmstrasse Palace, but the many rooms were now deserted and dead, like a noble old town house whose owner had retired to the country seat. Several bombs had fallen on it in the meantime, and the ancient structure was badly damaged. It contained countless ante-chambers and vestibules, staircases and steps which seemed to be there only to make human contact more difficult. Hitler's library was on the first floor, with his office, his bedroom and Eva Braun's apartment. There was a very large and very splendid reception room which Hitler claimed to have saved from destruction. 'The Old Gentleman [which was the nickname for Marshal von Hindenburg] received me in that room when I was named Chancellor. He said "Hitler, if you can, stand as close as possible to the walls. The floor is very weak." The whole place was falling into ruin because he'd never done any repair work.' Hitler had had the ceilings rebuilt, but a bomb had fallen directly onto that reception room and it had been abandoned.

The first floor was reached by three staircases. Opposite Hitler's office, several steps led to a corridor which contained a room for his entourage. It was known as the Steps Room, and it was the place where we spent most of our time. It was also used as a waiting room for the aides-de-camp and even as a bedroom for unexpected visitors. Next to this lived Schaub and Dr Dietrich, the Chief Press Officer, and then came a room for Gruppenführer Albrecht, Hitler's permanent aide-de-camp in Berlin. Further down the same passage were new rooms for Dr Morell, Colonel von Below, General Bergdorf and Heinrich Hoffmann, Hitler's accredited photographer.

On the ground floor the layout was the same, with an office for the housekeeper, Hausintendant Kannenberg, a small dining room for employees, the valets' bedrooms, a medicine cupboard, a bathroom and shower room, the laundry and the linen store.

Also on the ground floor, directly below the Führer's rooms, were the state rooms. The enormous hall still contained some of its fine furniture, carpets and pictures. An antechamber connected this to the large saloon and the Ladies Chamber. On the left were a cinema and a concert hall, from which three large doors led directly out to the Chancellery park.

The winter garden was undoubtedly the most beautiful room in the building. Built separately, it ran the whole length of the park, onto which it opened through enormous bay windows. Sadly, it could no longer really be called a winter garden, since its flowers and tropical plants had long since disappeared. At each of its semi-circular ends stood a large round table, used for breakfast, or sometimes used by Hitler for briefing sessions with a restricted number of his general staff. Normally, though, these meetings were held in his enormous office in the New Chancellery.

All these mighty buildings, deserted for so long, were now filled with people and life once again.

The Führer made a good recovery from the operation on his vocal chords. I didn't know whether it had been performed in a private clinic, or simply in the Führer's room, and we didn't see him for about three days. Then he appeared out of the blue one breakfast time. There had been an air-raid alert and Hitler had got up unusually early, woken by the sirens. Being at a loose end until the time for his briefing session, he'd felt like some company and had heard our voices.

In the twinkling of an eye the cigarettes went out and the windows were flung open. Most of us hadn't seen Hitler since his operation, and Dr Stumpfegger, the new doctor who had replaced Dr Brandt, had hardly met the Führer before. He was so flustered that in jumping to his feet to make his salute he upset his teacup and blushed furiously, pitifully embarrassed.

The Führer spoke in a low voice because he wasn't allowed to speak at full volume for a week. We too began to whisper, until Hitler pointed out that, even though he couldn't speak very well, his hearing was perfect and there was no need to humour him. We burst out laughing, and Hitler laughed too; the atmosphere became much more relaxed. He told us his great disappointment about Blondi: she wasn't expecting puppies after all. 'She's got very fat,' Hitler said, 'and she looks as if she could give birth soon, but I think she's put on so much weight because she's been given too much to eat and she hasn't got the chance to run about so much any more.' Hitler was wondering whether they should try again.

One after another, everyone left the table to go about their duties: the officers had to prepare the daily briefing session, while the Chief Press Officer and his deputy had to read the day's dispatches. After a while Frau Christian, Dr Stumpfegger and I were left alone with the Führer. We talked about Christmas, and asked him whether we'd be staying in Berlin over the festivities. He shook his head: 'I must leave for the Western Front, so we'll probably be at the Adlerhorst HQ, in the Taunus.' I took advantage of the occasion to ask if I could have a few days off to spend Christmas with my family. Frau Christian would stay, since in any case her husband would be wherever Hitler was. He agreed. Christmas was close, scarcely four weeks away, and we four were about to begin preparing the long list of presents and messages that the Führer sent every year. 'Yes, Christmas should be a family occasion,' Hitler murmured sadly. 'Eva has been writing me pressing letters, trying to get me to go to the Berghof at the end of the year. She insists I need rest after the assassination attempt and my operation. But I think Gretl is really behind it: she wants her Hermann!'

Eva's sister had married Hermann Fegelein on 3 June 1944. We were at the Berghof, and the wedding had been celebrated with much pomp and ceremony at an altitude of 6000 feet, in the Kehlstein mountain tea-house. Gretl was now expecting a baby in the spring. Amazingly enough, the handsome Hermann had managed to get into Eva's good graces – although perhaps it wasn't so surprising when you considered how entertaining Fegelein could be when he chose. Poor Eva, who was so young and fun-loving, led a very restricted and lonely life, so she was glad to have a brother-in-law with whom she could sometimes joke and dance without any danger of gossip.

But Hitler wouldn't be budged: when it was a question of 'duty' all Eva's charms and all her most persuasive arguments were useless, and now he couldn't wait to be on the move again. 'After spending so long in the east,' he said, 'it's essential for me to go to the Western Front.' Berlin had only been a brief halt, a two-week respite.

I was lucky enough to leave for Bavaria earlier than I'd thought. Captain Baur, Hitler's pilot, had to take a plane from Berlin to Munich and I asked him to take me with him: he agreed readily. I didn't even have to worry about my little fox terrier since I could take her too; dogs were forbidden on wartime trains.

I filled an enormous suitcase with presents and items made

scarce and precious by the war, which my family and friends would relish. All I had to do was to go through the Führer's birthday presents, which we were allowed to do; I turned up countless objects which would be very useful to my mother, whose house had been bombed and who now lived in the small village of Breitbrunn on Lake Ammersee, not far from Munich. I dragged along with me the whole of my husband's wardrobe, forgetting that the plane would only take me as far as the airport and that I'd then be faced with getting to the village, which didn't even have a railway station. After endless trouble I managed to get to the nearest town and left my cases at the station there, then continued with one bag and my dog, mostly on foot. It was all made worthwhile by the happiness of my family, who hadn't expected me so soon. And there I was, with my loved ones, in front of a real Christmas tree, in the warm atmosphere of preparations for the festivities, surrounded by a few small family objects that my mother had managed to salvage from the disaster.

I imagined that Hitler must be at his Adlerhorst HQ, surrounded by his generals, far from the festival of love and reconciliation that everyone was celebrating despite the terrible distress many of them were in. I was a bit worried because our little lodging, with its corner kitchen, didn't even have a telephone for contact with the outside world, just a wireless set that barely managed to pick up broadcasts from Munich – and most of those were interrupted by a chilling signal which meant that enemy bombers were not far away.

Just before 8 January 1945, the date when I was supposed to be back at the Führer's GHQ, Munich suffered one of its heaviest bombing raids. From our village twenty-five miles away we could see the blood-red sky and the explosions of the high-calibre bombs, which threw a blinding white light over the town. The next day all communications with Munich were cut, the railway line was severely damaged and the telephone lines weren't working, but I had to get to Berlin. My mother was very worried, begging me to stay a few more days and talking of her premonitions of danger . . . but I had to go. Leaving behind my heavy suitcase, I hitched a lift on a lorry going to Munich, and travelled through the smoking ruins and the streets filled with crowds of desperate people until I reached the Führer's house in Prinzregentenplatz. I was given my ticket to Berlin and took the train that same evening, carrying away from that leave the most desolate images of the horror of war.

Johanna Wolf, who had also been to Munich for Christmas, had returned to Berlin a few days before and was waiting for me. We were supposed to take the train to the Führer's HQ, in the west this time, and it turned out to be a mail train that took me to a part of Germany I'd never seen. We arrived in the morning at a little snow-covered station in Hessen, an uninspiring place by the name of Hunger. Cars had been sent to take us to the Adlerhorst. We passed through Bad Nauheim, still asleep and deserted on that winter morning, and set off along a road covered in thick snow which led through the woods that flanked the mountain up to the well-camouflaged HQ. It was cleverly arranged: a number of small pillboxes were hidden amongst the trees, but beneath each one was a deeply buried, solid bunker. The rooms were small but better equipped than at the Wolfsschanze. The Führer occupied two slightly larger rooms in the deepest bunker.

The first day, I went for a walk in the surrounding area. Quite close by was a small town where Marshal von Rundstedt, then commander-in-chief of the western armies, had his HQ. Hitler hoped that his presence would restore the morale of the troops and he also intended to explore with von Rundstedt possible ways of stopping the American advance. All day long there was incessant activity around the Führer's bunker, where the conference went on for hour after hour. We didn't see Hitler until the evening meal, when he seemed well rested and much fresher than in Berlin. I told him about the big bombing raid on Munich. He listened to my description and then said, 'These outrages will be over in a few weeks. Our new planes are coming off the production lines, and when they're ready the Allies will think twice before going into action over the territory of the Reich.'

The next day we were having tea as usual and Blondi was lying at her master's feet. After a while I saw that she was trying to attract Hitler's attention, but he hadn't noticed. Obviously she needed to go outside, for urgent reasons, and I plucked up courage to say, 'I think that Blondi really needs to go outside, *mein Führer.*' It was Blondi who reacted first to my words, jumping up and wagging her tail, bounding to the door, pushing the handle with her paw and throwing herself at the door while Hitler rang the bell to summon someone. 'It's amazing,' I said, 'how much pleasure one can give an animal with a little thing like that.' Hitler smiled, then said after a moment, 'Not just to an animal. Believe me, you've no idea how much pleasure it can give a man, too.

Before the war I used to go on long car journeys across the country with my party comrades. Once, I went to open a stretch of motorway near Magdeburg. When my line of cars was recognised, a huge number of cars joined the procession and it was impossible to escape for a moment alone in the woods along the roadside. So we kept going for hours without stopping. When we got to the place where the ceremony was to be held, both sides of the road were lined with delegates from all the party organisations: the Hitler Youth, the Union of German Girls, the SS and all the others. I knew that the party had a lot of different sections, but there seemed to be too many! Behind me Brückner and Schaub were suffering agonies, their teeth clenched. I had to stand there, saluting and smiling for hours. . . .'

Just then Schaub, who'd been listening to the story with delight, interrupted to say, 'Do you remember the Elephant, where you lived in Weimar, sir . . . ?'

'Oh, yes,' Hitler laughed, 'that's another terrible story. I often used to go to Weimar and I always stayed at the Hotel Elephant; a very old place but beautifully kept. I always had the same room there, which didn't have a toilet even though it had running water. The toilet was at the end of a long passage, and when I left my room for a pressing call of nature there was always someone who spotted me and spread the news. So when I left the toilet I found myself in the midst of a crowd of people shouting "Heil Hitler" and clapping. I had to raise my arm and salute them in reply, but it was very embarrassing in the circumstances.'

Chatting away in this vein, we could forget for a short while the disastrous news coming from all fronts. In fact, I never did get to visit the western HQ because Hitler was impatient to return to Berlin and keep an eye on events at the Eastern Front. He would really have liked to have been on both fronts at once – on the western one where the Anglo-American troops were advancing rapidly, and on the eastern one where the Russian armies would soon threaten Berlin. We joked that Berlin was the 'ideal spot for his headquarters, as it would soon be possible to travel from the Eastern to the Western Front by subway'.

16

'Red Roses Bring You Happiness'

January 1945 was my twenty-fourth month in the Führer's service. Since that fateful day of 20 July 1944 his state of health had steadily deteriorated. The Russians were getting closer and closer, and Hitler had decided on a hasty reinforcement of the Reich Chancellery.

On the 15th his entire staff – secretaries, orderlies, aides-de-camp and military advisers – set out by train for Berlin. We arrived in the evening. All building work on the enormous bunker in the heart of the Chancellery had been completed. A network of small apartments, dining rooms and conference halls, three storeys in all, was now buried in the ground with only a three-foot-high concrete wall still visible from the outside. The whole thing was protected by six-foot-thick concrete walls. It had been designed as an air raid shelter, but soon became a permanent residence for Hitler.

We secretaries and the Chancellery staff still lived in the Hermann-Goering-strasse, which led from the Potsdamer Platz to the Brandenburg Gate and was bordered on one side by the Chancellery park.

February 1945 was cold and wintry, and the snow-covered park looked desolate. In the bunker, though, it was warm: neither daylight nor weather penetrated the depths of the war's underground control centre. But the German people suffered terribly from hunger and cold. The enemy's bombs started horrifying conflagrations – fires of destruction rather than of warmth. On all sides the front line was retreating closer to Berlin, and the bombing raids were getting worse and worse.

I used to go for occasional walks in the grounds of the zoo nearby, to give my little dog, Foxl, and myself some fresh air and exercise, but on one of these walks I lost him. I had thrown him a snowball which he chased after in his usual lively way, but the obedient, faithful animal never came back to me. I had seen people gathering wood in the grounds, searching under the bomb-shattered trees for a few scraps of branches to put in their cold stoves, and I'm sure my well-nourished little dog became a welcome addition to the meagre contents of their cooking pot. I was sick at heart and searched all day for my dog. In this fraught period he was the only creature with whom I shared love, tenderness and a sense of belonging. But I could understand why the poor hungry people did what they must have done, and I consoled myself with the knowledge that Foxl's death had at least served some useful purpose.

A short while afterwards a heavy air raid destroyed our accommodation in the Hermann-Goering-strasse. The park, too, was becoming more and more a scene of devastation. We took the few personal belongings which we managed to salvage into the underground bunker in the Voss-strasse, where we were allotted a room with a couple of camp beds.

There were bombing raids on Berlin every evening now, so we all took to dining in Hitler's small living room inside his bunker. To get there involved following a tortuous route through his personal kitchen and down an interminable corridor to a heavy iron gate; through the gate, another corridor led us between the machine rooms, the heating and ventilation shafts, the toilets and the orderlies' rooms, before another armoured gate finally led into Hitler's bunker. The last part of the corridor had been designed as a waiting room. A wide red carpet covered the tiled floor and elegant chairs had been placed along the walls. Some valuable paintings had been brought down from Hitler's apartments in the Chancellery. The entrance to his office was on the left, beyond a small anteroom and covered by a curtain. The office was oppressively small, not more than nine by twelve feet, with a low ceiling and ordinary everyday furniture. On the right of the office a door led into Hitler's bedroom, to which there was no access from the corridor. On the left of the bedroom was a bathroom and a tiny dressing room which led through into what became Eva Braun's bedroom. Also leading off Hitler's bedroom was a small briefing room.

Hitler only went up to ground level occasionally, for brief periods, to let Blondi out, and then returned grim-faced to his dungeon. But he did come over to the bunker in the Voss-strasse, where a large, lovingly assembled model of the city of Linz had been set up in one of the rooms. There he stood with Speer and his entourage and had the plans for the aggrandisement of his beloved home town explained to him. He wanted to found a great gallery containing the most valuable paintings from his collection – Linz would become the jewel of Austrian cities. I took it as a small sign of hope that he was thinking in terms of a future, for I could not imagine that it was no more than a desire to escape from the horrors of reality that had turned his mind once again to his favourite subject.

During these weeks we secretaries were only rarely asked to take any dictation: practically our sole function was to comfort and entertain. But I do remember one piece of dictation from those days. An appeal to the defence forces of Berlin, it ended with the bombastic words: '. . . Berlin shall remain German, Vienna shall be German again, and Europe shall never be Russian!' It was difficult to believe.

Allied bombing raids had by now reduced most of Berlin to ashes and rubble. Hardly any public transport was still running, and people had sought refuge in the tunnels of the underground railway. There was no longer any opportunity to go and wander round the city – Hitler did not allow us to go any distance from the bunker. But in any case there was nothing to buy, and I was still able to contact my only friends in Wilmersdorf by telephone.

The battle fronts were drawing threateningly closer, and conferences on the military situation had turned into hectic attempts to save Berlin. The atmosphere in the bunker was characterised by desperate efforts to maintain a tiny spark of hope in life. No one wanted to be alone – everyone sought the companionship of others. We looked for human company, and yet none of us expressed his or her true innermost feelings. We talked of trivial matters, distracted ourselves, consoled ourselves with memories, thought of our families at home, and deadened our fear and doubt with alcohol, cigarettes and silly chatter – and yet each of us was in themselves quite alone.

The Russian advance continued at a thundering rate, and in late January we heard that they had crossed the East Prussian border. Appalling news came from the occupied towns and villages: children massacred, women raped. When we gathered for tea in the evenings Hitler's eyes were wild as he showed us photos from the Eastern Front – nothing but death and despair. He swore vengeance and let his fury against the Russians explode. 'These aren't men,' he'd shout, 'they're wild animals from the steppes of Asia. The war I'm waging against them is the battle for the dignity of the peoples of Europe. They're going to pay for this – no price is too high for our final victory. We must remain inflexible, and fight these savages with all the means at our disposal.'

One February lunchtime he complained to Christa Schroeder: 'I am lied to on all sides.' He could rely on no one, he said, and if anything happened to him Germany would be without a Führer. His successor, Goering, had lost the sympathy of the people because of the terrible bombing raids by the Allies, which he had promised would never happen. Hitler then apologised for talking politics at lunch, and said: 'Rack your brains again and tell me who my successor is going to be. This is a question that I keep on asking myself, without ever getting an answer.'

On 18 March Speer protested against the 'scorched earth' policy which was now being carried out on the Führer's orders. But Hitler said bitterly, 'If the war is lost the people will be lost too. It is not necessary to worry about what the common people will need for basic survival. On the contrary, it is best for us to destroy even those things. For this nation has proved to be the weaker, and the future belongs to the stronger eastern nation, the Soviet Union. In any case, only those who are inferior will remain after this struggle, for the good have already been killed.'

His spirits were raised shortly after this by Eva Braun's arrival in Berlin. Hitler had ordered her to stay at the Berghof, in relative safety, but she announced to her friends that she had to return to her man's side, no matter what. She told them that death no longer mattered and that she had to share the fate of the one she loved. Hitler pretended to be angry at her sudden appearance and made a show of scolding her, but all that first evening he repeated how proud he was of Fräulein Braun's devotion.

In the next few weeks, Eva began to forge a closer relationship with me, sometimes accompanying me for walks in the park. Neither her sisters nor any of her girlfriends were in the locality, and she was very lonely. She thought that I perhaps knew more than she did about the real state of the war, for she avoided bothering Hitler with her questions and fears.

I had to disappoint her. Even we secretaries knew no more about the situation than what Hitler expressed at mealtimes or while we were drinking tea with him in the evenings. Over and over again he repeated, with a serious expression on his face, that the decisive moment would be in Berlin. But we could see that he was weighed down with worries, and no one dared ask him if he continued to believe that Germany would win. He still sought to relieve the tension with sociable chatter, and nothing that he said suggested that in his heart of hearts he had no more hope.

On Easter Sunday all resistance to the Allied troops in the Ruhr had collapsed, and Hitler was forced to face the reality of total defeat. But he did his utmost to instill in us the hope of the last-minute miracle – the miracle of the new weapons! 'The decisive battle will be won in Berlin,' he assured a dubious audience. Incredibly, many of the soldiers were heartened by Hitler's words, and even the majority of civilians still kept their faith in him.

On 20 April, Hitler's fifty-sixth birthday, I did not feel remotely festive. The first Russian tanks had reached the outskirts of Berlin and the thunder of their artillery could easily be heard from the Chancellery. However a hundred or so officials and party followers from all over the Third Reich had come to greet the Führer, to shake his hand and swear their loyalty. Many tried to persuade him to leave the city.

'*Mein Führer*, the city will soon be surrounded and you will be cut off from the south. There is still time to withdraw to Berchtesgaden from where you can command the southern armies.'

Hitler shook his head, bluntly turning down their suggestions. However he did indicate that he was ready to move all the dispensable staff, ministries and departments to the south. Perhaps I would be going with them, I thought.

In the afternoon he went out into the park to decorate members of the Hitler Youth with the Iron Cross, for their bravery. They were still children but had managed to distinguish themselves in the struggle against Russian tanks. At their age, I was still playing with dolls. Does Hitler really intend to rely on this defence, I asked myself?

In the evening we sat packed together in the small study. I was dressed in a very unfestive manner, since all my clothes were dirty and I didn't know where or how I should wash them, or even whether I ever will. Hitler was unusually quiet and withdrawn. Frau Christian and I exchanged glances and finally plucked up the courage to ask him whether he intended to leave Berlin.

'No, I can't,' he answered. 'If I did, I would feel like a lama turning an empty prayer wheel. I *must* bring about the resolution here in Berlin – or else go under.'

141

We said nothing. The schnapps with which we were toasting Hitler had an insipid taste. Now he had said it: he no longer believed in victory. Dear God, let something happen. Can't Berlin be saved? I do not want to go under.

It was not at all late but Hitler retired to his room and the birthday gathering broke up. Eva Braun accompanied Hitler into his room but she came back later with a restless fire burning in her eyes. She was wearing a magnificent new dress of silver-blue brocade. Hitler had not even noticed it; neither had he noticed that the four young women who were sitting at his dinner table that evening were desperate to live.

I think Eva Braun was just as afraid as I was, but neither of us admitted it. She wanted to celebrate one last time, although there was nothing left to celebrate: to dance, drink, forget. . . . I joined her. Enough of the bunker! The heavy ceiling pressed down on the soul and the walls were so cold and white.

Eva Braun took everyone she met with her up into the old living room on the first floor of the Führer's apartment, which was still standing. The beautiful furniture was all down in the bunker, but the large round table was still there and it had been laid out in a festive manner once more. Even *Reichsleiter* Bormann had left Hitler's side and abandoned his command post. Fat Theo Morell, Hitler's personal physician, had come out of the safety of his bunker, despite the continual rumble of artillery. Someone had brought a gramophone, but only one record – a popular pre-War hit called 'Red Roses Bring You Happiness'. It is a very catchy tune and everyone started dancing. We drank champagne and laughed loudly, but it was a very hollow kind of laughter. I joined in, but there was a big lump in my throat.

Suddenly a sharp explosion shook the building, making the windows tremble; then the telephone rang and someone hurried to take the call and write down the message; someone else received some important reports.

I suddenly felt as though I was going to be sick at any moment – not because of the champagne, but because of the misery in my heart. The muffled roar of the artillery seemed to become louder than the laughter and the music, so that I could no longer ignore it. I discreetly left that last party and crept through the labyrinth of passages in the cellars and bunkers until I reached the Chancellery, where, in a large store room in the bunker, there was a bed waiting for me. I wanted to fall asleep and not wake up until it was all over.

By the next day all the guests who had come to celebrate Hitler's birthday had left and were heading south. Ribbentrop tried to enlist Eva's help in persuading Hitler to go with them. 'Eva,' he implored, 'you are the only one who can persuade him to leave. Tell him that you will not leave Berlin unless he comes with you. You will be performing a great service to Germany.' Eva told me that she replied: 'I will not say one word on the subject to the Führer. He alone will decide. If he thinks it right that he should stay in Berlin, then I will remain here with him.'

Convoys of cars and several aeroplanes were speeding south to safety. Johanna Wolf and Christa Schroeder, the two senior secretaries, were among the passengers. Johanna was crying as she said goodbye, because Hitler had been her boss for twenty-five years and she felt sure that she would never see him again. As they left, the Führer solemnly shook hands with everyone.

In the afternoon of 21 April, Hitler learned that Russian troops were approaching Berlin and he ordered a last assault by all the able men available. Every tank, every weapon of whatever kind was to be used in the battle. The bunker echoed with the sound of hand grenades and mortars, and with the Führer's voice yelling orders at his generals in the briefing rooms. Gerda Christian and I sat anxiously in the corridor, where we were joined by Martin Bormann's secretary, Else Krueger. We could only wait. The generals emerged from the small briefing room, their faces scarlet. Hitler went off to find his puppies and sat on a narrow bench in the corridor with a puppy on his knee, watching the men come and go and occasionally firing orders at them.

The tension was almost unbearable. All at once, Eva emerged from her bedroom and announced that she wanted to go for a stroll in the Chancellery gardens and breathe some fresh air. Shells had ripped up the lawns and broken great branches off the trees. Along the wall, piles of *Panzerfausten* – wooden-handled grenades – were arranged in perfect order. Were they to be used as ammunition in the final battle? We left the Chancellery gardens and crept into the park of the Foreign Ministry through the broken walls.

Hitler had at last allowed the women to practise shooting with a pistol in the park. Before that, when Gerda Christian and I had asked if it wouldn't be wise for us to learn to use a pistol, he had replied with a laugh: 'Ladies, I wouldn't want to die at the hands of one of my secretaries! Shoot with your eyes, that's enough for

143

me!' Then, a few days ago, he had changed his mind and allowed us our pistol practice.

The park was so peaceful. It was springtime: leaves were appearing on the trees, birds were singing, crocuses and snow-drops bloomed in the grass. Behind a bush we discovered a beautiful bronze statuette, a naiad amongst the flowers. It seemed strangely out of place in our hopeless, wartorn surroundings, like a goddess in the midst of hell.

We had taken Eva's two dogs with us and they ran wildly all over the park, overjoyed at last to be allowed some freedom. Gerda and I sat down on a rock and lit cigarettes. To our great surprise, Eva asked if she could have one too, saying, 'Desperate situations call for desperate measures.' When she finished her cigarette she took a tiny pillbox from her handbag and started sucking a menthol tablet so that Hitler would not notice the smell of smoke on her breath. At that moment, the air raid siren began to howl and we had to rush back into the bunker.

Hitler was still sitting on a bench in the corridor near his quarters, talking to Goebbels and Martin Bormann about the imminent assault on the advancing Russian forces. He seemed much more vigorous, and as we approached, he rose to greet us. Normal protocol had been abandoned as the 'inner circle' was now so small, and we were much less tied by convention. Hitler invited us to sit down on the bench. At last, I thought, we would learn whether he was going to leave Berlin and go south to Bavaria, or stay here to the bitter end.

Eva sat next to him. 'Tell me,' she said, 'do you know that bronze statuette in the park? It's absolutely enchanting. It would fit perfectly in my garden, near the pond. Would you buy it for me if we get away from Berlin?' She looked at him pleadingly. I have never seen an expression on Hitler's face such as he had then, so completely unlike that of the dictator or the Führer. He held her hands and said, 'But my dear child, I don't know who owns it. It's probably state property, so I can't buy it and put it in a private garden.'

'Yes,' she replied, 'but you could make an exception if you repelled the Russians and liberated Berlin.' This twisted logic made Hitler laugh, and the subject was changed.

Eva pointed to a few red and black stains on Hitler's uniform. 'Look at that,' she said. 'You can't wear this coat any more. It's a mess. You mustn't try and be like old Fritz [Frederick the Great] in everything he did, including walking around looking as though you have no one to take care of you.'

Hitler protested, 'But it's my working coat. Do you expect me to wear an apron when I'm bending over maps and using coloured pencils?' Actually, Eva was being a bit unfair because Hitler's obsession with neatness and cleanliness was practically clinical. If he had been patting the dogs, for instance, he would never shake hands with anyone without going to wash his hands first.

This idle talk was interrupted again by the air raid sirens. Hitler went to listen to the radio broadcast. The announcer said: 'A huge wave of aeroplanes is now penetrating the Reich. Berlin will once more be heavily bombed.'

17

The Military Viewpoint: Otto Günsche Talks

Otto Günsche explains Hitler's military position and intentions during the final month of his life.

Right up until the last few days of April 1945, Hitler never admitted in my presence or to any of his entourage that the war was lost. For the previous six months he had adopted a special tactic at the daily conferences on the war situation of trying to compensate for the disastrous news from the fronts by stressing the disagreements and disputes between the different Allied forces. He would read to us from the news and dispatches his press officers obtained for him from foreign sources. Admittedly it did seem as though there were crippling difficulties in the relationships between the Allies – particularly between the western Allies and the Russians. Hitler placed great weight on these reports and tried to use them to bolster the morale of his generals and the other officers present. But, of course, what really interested them were the precise details of the military situation.

In fact, the first time that I heard the Führer utter any negative sentiments whatsoever at these briefing meetings was at the end of April 1945 when the Oder front collapsed. That was the meeting at which he announced that he could no longer continue to direct operations and that he intended to stay in Berlin. Before that he had never really admitted the seriousness of the situation, and even then when someone asked him, 'Can we still win the war?' he replied, 'The war must be won!' – an answer that took no account of the reality of the situation at the fronts. At these formal conferences he never expressed the idea that the war might be lost.

He had for some time been arguing with General Guderian about the best distribution of the armed forces. Guderian thought it essential to maintain the full weight of the northern defences against the Russians along the Vistula. But Hitler had ordered several divisions, including the 6th Panzer Armoured Division, to advance towards Hungary. His sights were set on the vital Hungarian oilfields in the Lake Balaton region, and he used this argument to counter anyone who tried to convince him that the most important thing was to stop the Russians taking Berlin. 'If I couldn't even hold that line of defence [along the Vistula],' Hitler said, 'then the war really would be lost.' But he believed that would never happen if his generals stood firm and held their positions.

Naturally, I had doubts myself but I simply could not let them take shape in my mind. Events obviously indicated more and more that we might lose the war, but I could not admit the possibility. That's a normal reaction for an officer, and I think it was the attitude of all those in our little group in the bunker. Perhaps people living outside in the towns and cities that had been so heavily bombarded had a more accurate picture of the situation. Inside the bunker we knew that the Russians were getting closer and closer, but we never thought of surrender – just of fighting on to the end. It was not even a conscious decision, but the only possible way to think.

Reinforcements were made to the Chancellery defences and the Führer's bunker during the last few days of April, but they should not be interpreted as a last-ditch attempt by Hitler to fight for the capital and change the course of events. The main reinforcements to the bunker had been completed months earlier and there were just a few modifications made in April. It was like a small fortress in the middle of a ruined city, but not a fortress from which a battle was to be fought. Hitler believed that Berlin would be defended on the Oder and he had concentrated his troops, equipment and anti-aircraft guns along there. There were not many troops in Berlin itself, just disparate collections of foreigners, prisoners of war and a few troops like the French 'Waffen SS' from the Charlemagne Division that became one of the last defenders of the city.

Hitler had placed all his hopes in two men: the young General Walter Wenck and General Felix Steiner, both members of the

SS. He spent his last days desperately trying to get in touch with
Steiner, who was in the region of Oranienburg, just north of
Berlin. The plan was to create a new line of defence which was
to be held at all costs. Wenck's army was supposed to break
through the Russian lines and march on to Berlin, and the
Luftwaffe were supposed to provide support from the air.
However, the Luftwaffe had no planes left and Steiner had an
army but no more ammunition. When the order from Hitler to
march on Berlin finally got through, Steiner decided that he didn't
want to become trapped in the capital and the attack never took
place.

Hitler transferred his last hopes to General Wenck, and never
stopped expecting him to perform a miracle. The last document
he signed was a telegram addressed to the Wehrmacht General
Staff, which had just moved to Doblin. It was received at 11 p.m.
on 29 April, and it consisted of five questions, four of which
concerned Wenk:

1. Where are Wenck's advance units?
2. When are they going to attack?
3. Where is 9th Army?
4. Where does it intend to effect a breakthrough?
5. Where are Holst's advance units?

There was no need to wait for a reply. By one o'clock in the
morning on 30 April, Hitler had learned that Wenck's 12th Army
was stuck and could not undertake a march on Berlin; the 9th
Army was surrounded, and Holst's forces were reduced to
defensive positions.

Hitler feared that the Russians might make their final push into
the city on May Day. At about half past three in the afternoon
on 30th April, with Evan Braun at his side, he took his own life.

18

Escape from the Bunker

Frau Junge takes up her story again on 1 May 1945.

Returning to our quarters, we destroyed all our identity papers. I left behind my money, food and clothes, taking only plenty of cigarettes, a few photographs, my pistol and the cyanide capsule. I was sure that I would never get through the Russian frontlines alive. The other women had bags and bundles. We were impatient to get out and make our way across the city, where most of the buildings had been razed to the ground and many were on fire.

The first party left. My three women friends and myself, some soldiers of Hitler's special guard, Otto Günsche, General Mohnke, who was in charge of defending the Chancellery and the centre of Berlin, Walter Hewel and Admiral Voss slipped past the numerous men waiting in the underground corridors. We climbed half-destroyed stairs and scrambled through holes in walls, until at last we reached the Wilhelmplatz, which was dimly lit by the moon. The carcass of a dead horse lay in the street, and dozens of starving people had emerged from the shelters and were cutting it up for food. In the distance we could hear continuous gunfire. We reached the subway in front of the Kaiserhof Hotel and found the hotel completely destroyed. Down the stairs in the dark tunnel of the subway, wounded and homeless people and exhausted soldiers lay stretched out on the ground. We walked along the track and at length reached Friedrichstrasse station, the end of the line, where we emerged. We managed to cross the railway bridge very stealthily, but soon afterwards we heard rifle fire. Hundreds of snipers were shooting at the party immediately behind us.

We crawled through cellars and houses and slipped down dark, unfamiliar streets until we found an empty cellar where we slept for a couple of hours. When we started out again, Russian tanks were blocking our route, so we returned to the cellar and spent the night there. At dawn the shooting had stopped and it was quiet again, so we resumed our flight.

We finally reached a shelter that had once been part of a brewery. The square outside was all lit up and we could see masses of Russian tanks. Mohnke and Günsche sat down in a corner and started to write reports. Ambassador Hewel lay down on a bench, absolutely silent, and stared at the ceiling. He did not want to go any further. Two soldiers entered carrying General Rattenhuber and they placed him on a makeshift bunk. He had been wounded in the legs, and was incoherent with fever; a doctor who was in the shelter took care of him. Rattenhuber took out his pistol and placed it at his side in readiness. He intended to kill himself rather than be taken prisoner, but this was not to be.

A general came into the bunker and spoke to the leader of our party. We learned that we were holed up in the last centre of resistance in Berlin. The Russians had just encircled the brewery and had ordered those inside to surrender.

Mohnke finished writing his report just one hour before the Russians' ultimatum expired. He turned to the women of the party and said: 'You must help us now. Since the men are all in uniform, we don't stand a chance of escaping, but you can try to get out of Berlin and go north to Admiral Dönitz's headquarters and give him this report.'

I didn't want to be part of this foolhardy scheme, but Frau Christian and the two other women persuaded me to go ahead. We took off our steel helmets, our pistols and our military jackets, shook hands with the men and left.

Members of the Volkssturm, the people's militia, and the Todt Organization had already thrown down their weapons and surrendered. In the brewery courtyard, Russian soldiers were distributing cigarettes and schnapps to those who had surrendered. We managed to walk through all the confusion as if we were invisible. We were right in the middle of a square surrounded by victorious Russian soldiers. At last I could have a good cry!

The streets of Berlin had a nightmarish look. Germany's most-bombed city was blackened by soot and pockmarked by thousands of craters. Whole apartment blocks were devastated; what had once been streets were now pitted trails that wound through mountains of rough stones; everywhere windowless, roofless buildings gaped up at the sky.

Crowds of people were laboriously trying to make their way through the rubble. Old and young, women and children, and a few men carrying small packs, pushed rusty carts or prams full of assorted belongings. The Russian soldiers did not seem to be paying much attention to these desperate human beings. From time to time, however, a patrol armed with machine guns would push forward with a group of prisoners. We could hear the uninterrupted rumbling of the heavy guns. Here we were, four women, looking like hopeless refugees: we had no papers, no money and no food. I had some cigarettes. Frau Christian, I noticed later, had been more prudent. She was wearing a dress that she had tucked into her trousers, and I think she had a little food and some cash in a small bag.

We were supposed to be heading north to find Hitler's appointed successor, Admiral Dönitz, but we didn't know where to look for him. Moreover, we quickly realized that we would be better travelling in a roundabout direction, taking streets that did not appear to be controlled by Russian patrols. Soon we split up. Frau Christian and Fräulein Krueger went to a water supply point, hoping to find some lodging vouchers there. Fräulein Manziarly, who was wearing strange clothing that made her look too much like a soldier, wandered over towards a group of women.

Suddenly the shooting resumed. I dived for shelter under a porch, and when it was over my companions had disappeared. I was all alone now and I set off walking, occasionally joining other groups of refugees. At last I found myself on a country road, and I stopped for a nap in a barn. There was no one there, as the farmers had all fled.

The next day I encountered more refugees, all of them heading north in an attempt to reach the part of Germany that was occupied by the British. Among those refugees was a nice woman, Kate Düsler, with whom I became friendly. Her husband had been a member of the SS and her children had been evacuated from Berlin. Now at least I didn't feel so lonely, but we still had nothing to eat, and we were filthy and exhausted, despite managing to grab some sleep in barns. We were hoping to reach the 'green frontier', away from the cities and the Russians, but we never succeeded.

We did reach the Elbe, however, and for a while we debated

whether we would be able to swim to the other side where the British were, but I was too weak to try. Once I saw a familiar face: seated at the door of a farmhouse was Erich Kempka, Hitler's chauffeur, wearing a soldier's old rags and looking like a tramp. He said he was waiting for dark, when he planned to cross the Elbe.

Kate and I walked for more than ten days, perhaps fifteen, eating anything the farmers were willing to spare. Sometimes we stole a few potatoes, and once in a while a farmer would offer us a meal.

One night, as we rested in a barn, I felt I couldn't keep my secret any longer. I was so unhappy and so desperate to open my heart to someone that I told Kate who I was. Of course, it was sheer foolishness, but I couldn't help myself. Kate was most understanding. Later, when I was betrayed, I knew she was not the informer. Some other refugees had joined us and had shared the barn that night, and I believe that one of them overheard me.

After a lot of thought, Kate suggested that we should return to Berlin. It seems hard to understand why we went back to the Russian-held sector when we could have found safety in the British zone, but we would never have had the strength to swim across the Elbe. 'My home is in Berlin,' said Kate, 'and maybe things will be less chaotic now.' I agreed with her. So we walked back to Berlin with a few other women and two or three men. The roads were crowded with people who were now going back to the capital. It was as if the whole of Germany was going from one place to another, in every direction, and that everyone had his or her own idea as to what was best to do. But one way or the other, nothing made sense anyway. At night we often heard the screams of women who were being raped by Russian soldiers, but we must have had a guardian angel because it never happened to us.

When we arrived in Berlin we went to Kate's house, where I had a bath and washed my clothes. I combed my hair and put on a dress that Kate had given me. At last I was a human being again, a woman, and I felt a little more secure. We even managed to obtain food cards.

But I was soon in trouble. One morning, while Kate was out, the doorbell rang and when I answered it a man and a woman were there.

The woman spoke poor German, with a heavy accent. I knew instinctively that they were going to arrest me. They told me to come along. I took a little jacket and a silk blouse that Kate had given me, and wrapped my cyanide capsule in a handkerchief. They took me to a Russian military office located in a private house. The man asked who I was and I decided that I might as well tell the truth. Immediately he got very excited, urged me to sit down and offered me some cocoa; he was happy to have caught such a rare fish! He was a young officer and didn't ask me any more questions, probably because he didn't know what to ask.

I was taken to another office, and this time was thoroughly searched. They called it a 'body search'. They checked my clothes, the linings, and even the stitching of my sleeves. I still had my cyanide capsule buried in my handkerchief, but they didn't find it. Pretending I had to blow my nose, I slipped the capsule into my mouth. Earlier, I had removed the metallic covering that protected it, but the glass was very fragile so I had to pretend to blow my nose again and hide it back in my handkerchief.

I was transferred to a series of jails, most of them in basements. In the Lichtenberg women's prison I originally had a cell to myself, but very soon it was filled with all kinds of female prisoners. One of them was a sixteen-year-old girl suspected of having been a member of Wehrwolf, a Nazi partisan group that had been formed towards the end of the war with the aim of conducting guerrilla warfare behind the Allied lines. She was a strange girl, totally unaware of the danger she was in. I remained in that prison for weeks without once being submitted to any questioning. But I knew that interrogations were going on and that was quite frightening. Every time the radios were turned up, I guessed they were giving somebody the third degree.

Somehow I managed to survive that imprisonment rather well. I had reached a state of calm acceptance. Of course I was locked up, but I didn't resent it, even when the Russian jailers shouted things like: 'You Krauts executed my wife, killed my children. . . .'

The nights were the worst; that was when the Russians took prisoners out for interrogation. On one of those nights I was taken to a villa where a high-ranking officer questioned me. For the first time I was asked some really pertinent questions.

'Where is Hitler?'

'He is dead,' I said. 'He committed suicide.'

They all screamed, 'You are a liar!' Finally, an officer allowed me to talk. The scene was nightmarish. We were in a bedroom with a four-poster bed in a corner and a mirror above it. An officer stood behind a table covered with a Persian rug. After I had told my story, I was sent back to my cell.

The prison was filling up now. At times, up to eight women shared my cell. The sixteen-year-old girl started a flirtation with a young man who I think was an interpreter. He came to visit her at night. Usually he bribed the warden and took her outside but once in a while they made love right there in the cell, ignoring our presence.

One day – I can't remember exactly when – I was taken out again and driven to another building and locked up in the basement. This was much better than my other cell, whose windows had been covered with rough boards and old rags. I spent a few weeks there before I was again called for questioning. The interpreter was a Russian officer who had a horse whip on his desk. Seated next to him was another officer. They asked me questions about Hitler's personal life. 'What did he do with Eva Braun? Was he really a vegetarian?' I had become quite unconcerned and answered all their questions as they asked them.

I still had my cyanide pill in my handkerchief. Before going to sleep, I had always put it in a pocket of my jacket so as not to crush it. The routine inspections at night were usually carried out quite carelessly, but one night they went to town, searching through everything and, sure enough, they found the pill. Now I was at their mercy. I no longer had the option of escape through death. The capsule had given me a sense of security and I'd always thought, 'You can threaten me, you can deport me to Russia, but you won't have me. I will always have the last word.' Now I truly was in their hands.

But despair gave way to a feeling of curiosity. What would happen next? Would I get lucky again? It was like Russian roulette; I became excited and intrigued.

There was a strange woman in my cell, who said she was a doctor. She had witnessed the discovery of my cyanide capsule and she told me: 'I know a quick and reliable way of committing suicide. It is absolutely painless. You tie a very tight knot around a finger until it literally dies. That causes blood poisoning. Then you untie the knot. Gangrene spreads into your body and death occurs soon after.' I decided that the time for testing this procedure had not yet arrived.

Again days and nights went by monotonously until one night, at the end of July, I was awakened abruptly. A man said, 'Come quickly and bring all your belongings!' Waiting for me in a car was a civilian who looked like one of the caricatures of Jews that were published regularly in *Der Stürmer*, Hitler's weekly anti-semitic magazine. He had a long, hooked nose, thick-lipped mouth and carbon-black curly hair. His name was Arkadi and he was an Armenian; he spoke perfect German, with no accent at all. He drove me to another villa, and led me to the first floor where a Russian officer was seated at a desk. The Armenian seemed to be more of an interpreter than anything else. Very gently he said, 'Sit down and tell me everything you know.'

The Armenian let me talk without interruption, noting down a sentence from time to time, but never really taking notes. The Russian officer remained silent, playing with a pencil. he didn't seem to be paying any attention to what I was saying. As I continued, I felt more and more relaxed. The interview lasted between two and two and a half hours. When I finished, the Armenian escorted me to my basement cell and shook my hand. It touched me deeply. Never since my arrest had anyone shown me such decency. They had only given me orders, bullying me, saying '*du*' (the familiar German pronoun, considered insulting when spoken to strangers and criminals) and, 'Woman, do this, do that.' Before locking me in, Arkadi said something strange: 'You must get out of here.' I looked at him wide-eyed, speechless.

A day or so later, he came to fetch me again. I'd had a horrid night. A badly wounded German officer had yelled and moaned deliriously all night long in the neighbouring cellar. Hearing him suffer so much completely destroyed me. When the Armenian arrived, I was in total despair. He took me into the interrogation room and said, 'Do precisely what I tell you.' He then showed me a piece of paper: 'You must sign this document.' He read it to me in German.

I was still disturbed by that frightful night and didn't under-stand the paper too well, except that it said that I pledged myself to tell the Red Army everything I knew about the people who were in the bunker.

I asked: 'Why should I sign this paper? I have already told you all I know.'

Once more he repeated: 'You should sign.'

I did as he asked. Then he took me back to the basement and left. When he returned the next morning he announced, 'Now you are free.'

It all happened like a dream. I couldn't believe it after all I had been through: the last days in the bunker, the sight of Berlin burning and destroyed, my escape, the prisons. In a daze, I followed him into the street. Two or three blocks away, we stopped in front of a house. He rang the bell, and a woman opened the door. Arkadi said, 'I belong to the Russian Command, and I want to requisition a bedroom.' She was a shy old spinster, a piano teacher. She said she had only one bedroom and Arkadi told her that I was to move in. There was a smaller room. I said it would be good enough for me. Arkadi told me, 'You are not allowed to leave the Soviet sector. You must report to me every day at noon, and I will take you to lunch.'

I was now comparatively free. I had my own little room and the old lady was terribly sweet. I simply lived from day to day. I wondered why Arkadi had been so kind to me. Did he plan to use me as a spy for the Russians? Did he think he could go to bed with me? I was young, blonde, blue-eyed and attractive. One day he had said, 'Just call me Arkadi.' What was it all about?

Never once did I see Arkadi in a Russian uniform. It was all very mysterious as far as I was concerned. Of course the war was over now, but it was difficult for me to accept the fact.

Every day at noon I went to the Command office. Arkadi was always waiting for me on the pavement. At the officers' mess, we ate the beetroot soup called *bortsch* and *kasha* – fine wheat grain, full of grease and very rich. It was very heavy on my stomach, and very hard to digest.

This lasted several days, during which time I grew more and more anxious. I still could not understand Arkadi's unusual behaviour. Our relationship was odd, to say the least. During our meals we normally only spoke of unimportant matters. One day I told him, 'I can't go on like this. I think I'll soon go crazy, and I would rather go back to jail unless you tell me what this is all about.'

He started to scream, 'But this is sheer madness! If you do that, you will be in for good! I must find a job for you.'

I was willing. December 1945 was approaching and I didn't have a winter coat or money or an identity card – and that was very serious in those days. People were being checked all the time. Without papers you were automatically arrested, and in my case it would have meant going through all sorts of examinations again and possibly exile to Russia.

Arkadi took me to a shop where he got me an identity card and a ration book for food, and drove me to the Berlin Charité hospital. He said, 'From now on you will work here.' At first I was employed in the registration office. I was on a payroll like the other employees.

By this time Berlin had been divided into four sectors by the Allies, and I began venturing closer to the British sector, which was adjacent to the Russian one. Sometimes I crossed secretly, usually on Sundays. I had friends who had been living there before the occupation, and I even spent a couple of weekends with them.

On New Year's Eve of 1945–6 I was celebrating with them when I fell seriously ill with diphtheria. I couldn't get to the Charité in the Russian sector, so I spent six weeks in a hospital in the British zone. When I finally returned to my bedroom in the old maid's apartment, I realized that nobody had been looking for me. My housekeeper and my colleagues at the Charité thought I had run away.

One morning, as I was walking near the office of the Russian Command, I saw Arkadi. He came towards me and, bypassing me, he whispered: 'We have a new commanding officer. Your files have disappeared.' He walked away casually as if I had been a perfect stranger.

I never saw him again. I wonder to this day why he was so kind. I had only one clue. One day, after I confided that I was worried about my future, he had replied, 'Don't think that I am your enemy. I am Armenian. Maybe some day you will rescue me.' Could this have meant that he was not a Communist, and that perhaps he was working for the Allies? Could he have been an American agent? I don't think I will ever know the truth. I never mentioned his name when I was arrested later by the Americans. At that time I had no idea what their relationship with the Russians was, and I feared exposing him.

When I returned to the Charité hospital, I was promoted to the job of nurse's aide. During that period it was almost impossible to travel; there was a tricky and dangerous crossing between Berlin and the other zones into which Germany had been divided because the city was an island in the middle of the Soviet zone. Early in 1946 I met a woman who worked at the railway station and she got me a ticket for Munich; the two of us set off together. A frontier runner was supposed to help us cross the border between the Russian and the US sectors, and after that we simply had to catch another train that would take us to Munich. Unfortunately it didn't work, and we were arrested, but there were so many people trying to do the same thing that it had become a routine matter. We were simply driven back to the Soviet sector – where we could start all over again.

This time, we went to a nearby village. A farmer showed us a path through the fields. At dawn, carrying knapsacks, we crossed the border near Cassel into the British zone. From there it was easy to take a train to Munich and then to Ammersee, about eighteen miles away, where my mother now lived. The three of us – my mother, my sister Inge and I – were at last reunited. It was Easter 1946.

About a week after Easter I was arrested again – this time by the Americans. A male friend of mine was going out with a secretary who worked at the CIC, the US Counter-Intelligence Corps. My friend innocently told her that he knew someone who had been one of Hitler's secretaries and she reported it to her chief. My friend realised he had made a mistake when his girl-friend began asking a lot of questions about me. He telephoned me to apologise for having behaved foolishly, but the damage had been done.

Once more I was put under arrest, but compared with what I had gone through with the Soviets, being arrested by the Americans was no problem. I was taken to Starnberg prison and kept there for three weeks. The Americans were very kind. I explained that I had already been arrested by the Russians, that I had escaped and had crossed the border illegally.

The Americans were quite fair. Instead of sending me to Nuremberg prison, where the Russians would certainly have claimed me again, I was transferred to Garmisch-Partenkirchen, fifty or so miles from Munich, where I was again questioned exhaustively. The Americans were most interested to learn about the last days in the bunker, since very little was known about Hitler's death. Eye-witness accounts were few and far between because most of the witnesses had been deported to Russia. The Americans wanted confirmation of what little they already knew. I told them everything.

19

A Soldier's Story: Otto Günsche's Escape and Imprisonment

Otto Günsche takes up his story on 1 May 1945.

Our escape from the bunker was organised and commanded by the highest-ranking officer present, General Mohnke. There was no question of a disorganised affair in which everyone went their own way. The decision to try to break out had been taken after General Krebs came back from the Russians' HQ and announced that his mission to negotiate a ceasefire had failed. The groups who were to attempt the escape were formed and given orders to set off towards the city centre. The exodus had been set for 20.00 hours. But in fact these turned out to be the last orders issued, and from that moment onwards we simply had to react according to circumstance and opportunity. Each group had to decide how best to make their way across the city, and whether or not to fight it out. Some people decided to wear civilian clothes – Axmann, Naumann, Kempka, for example – but others, like myself, kept their uniforms.

We were lucky enough to be the first out, and the Russians didn't see us. Gradually, despite the darkness, they noticed movements around the Chancellery, and later groups were caught in their fire.

We passed through subway tunnels until we got to the street in which the Friedrichstrasse station stood. The Russians often fired at us, but we were still together as a group. During the course of the night we'd managed to get as far as the Wettlingen district, to the north of the city, where we knew there was a restaurant in which we could shelter. Other groups who had been attacked had arrived before us, and there were dead and wounded who couldn't go any further.

There were several officers in the restaurant, army and Luftwaffe generals, and we drew up a plan for making our way through the Russian stranglehold. There were about two thousand people there, all wanting to get out of the besieged city, but naturally enough most of them preferred to find a way that did not involve fighting against hopeless odds. Besides, they were a very mixed bunch of people. It was hard to distinguish the combatants from the non-combatants; there were women and civilians too.

But the situation changed suddenly when the Russians sent negotiators with white flags to demand that we give ourselves up. They spoke to the generals, Mohnke amongst them, and told them that the German army had surrendered. We weren't sure whether to believe this. We couldn't see who could have signed a surrender, since the last person to have negotiated on the subject was General Krebs. Yet he was in our group, and we knew his attempt to obtain a ceasefire had failed and that he hadn't signed anything. So the generals replied that they wanted confirmation from authorised personnel, and the Russians suggested taking them to their command post. The generals agreed, including General Mohnke, who asked me to go with him. It was at the command post that we learnt that General Weidling, commander of the city of Berlin, had signed a surrender for the troops in the capital – the Berlin garrison, in other words – but not for the Wehrmacht as a whole. General Mohnke then replied that, as we weren't part of the Berlin garrison, the capitulation didn't apply to us, and the Russians said 'Show us where the rest of you are, or we'll shoot you now.'

All this had lasted some time, however, and when we returned we found a great change. The restaurant was practically empty and the soldiers had dispersed, perhaps having tried to find their own way out and fallen into the hands of the Russians. The four women with us – Frau Junge, Frau Christian, Frau Krueger and Fräulein Manziarly – had left earlier. The only people left from our group were Ambassador Hewel, another officer, and one of the doctors, Professor Schenk. As soon as we arrived, the Russians demanded: 'Put your hands up!' and took us prisoner.

That was the beginning of my imprisonment. As I'd become a sort of orderly officer to General Mohnke, I followed him into the first camp for generals, close to Berlin, where we were very well treated. This was the way the Russians usually treated senior officers. The regime wasn't particularly strict and there were certainly quite a few opportunities to escape. I thought about it, naturally. The Russians had no idea who I was, nor of my position on Hitler's staff. As far as they knew I was just another officer with the rank of major, like a thousand others, so I wasn't made the object of any special surveillance. But then something quite unforeseeable happened, something which ended badly for me and caused me to be deported to Russia. But I would probably have been deported anyway. . . .

In the same camp for generals was the commander of Berlin, General Weidling, who was regarded as an important witness, since the Russians were desperately keen to know exactly what had happened to Hitler. He told them Hitler had committed suicide, that his body had been burnt and that there couldn't be the slightest doubt that he was dead. They didn't really believe him. And as chance would have it, one day when they were in the middle of questioning one of us – General Weidling's aide-de-camp, I think – I happened to be walking down the corridor next to the office where the interrogation was taking place, and the door was open. I used to walk around the different parts of the camp as much as possible, reconnoitring a possible escape route. Just at that moment, never suspecting the harm he was about to do me, Weidling's aide-de-camp said to his interrogators: 'Look, ask that officer! He knows more about Hitler's death than anyone. He'll confirm it for you.'

From then on I became a very important person. They began to interrogate me, and one of the Russian officers asked me, in German, who I was. I replied that I was General Mohnke's aide-de-camp. He shouted: 'You're a liar!' I answered that it wasn't a lie; I certainly was, by then, the orderly officer to the General, but that didn't interest the Russians. I was immediately placed apart from the other inmates, and after a few days – I can't remember the date – we were assembled into a little group – Generals Mohnke, Weidling and Rattenhuber, and a few others as well – and put on a plane.

No one told us where we were going, but we guessed. The plane set off towards the east and it was a long flight, just about long enough for the journey to Moscow. As soon as we landed, we were taken to a prison where they proceeded to interrogate us; then, the next day, to the infamous Lubianka. From that day onwards, they never stopped questioning me on the same subject:

what happened to the Führer? However often I repeated that he'd killed himself and that his body had been burnt, in accordance with the orders he'd given me, it was impossible to convince them. At one point they even said I'd deliberately let myself be taken prisoner to put them on the wrong track! They were equally suspicious of the other witnesses, especially Captain Hans Baur, who told them the same story.

This lasted a very long time – a year, maybe, or a year and a half. They repeated the same questions over and over again, and I finally began to feel some internal satisfaction at the thought that they obviously hadn't been able to find the body. Later I asked some of the people who had been questioned, including the valet, Linge, about this: they had never been able to identify any remains of the corpse. A Russian author called Bezimensky later wrote a book which included the famous story of Hitler's jaw, which had supposedly been discovered and shown to his dentists and his dentist's assistant, both of whom were said to have recognised it. But I'm sure even that is not true: they probably reconstructed it from X-rays in the dentist's files.

It's true that I didn't see the bodies burnt right to the very end. I went back up to the Chancellery garden at one point, while they were still burning, and then returned to the bunker, where there were urgent jobs to attend to. People have said that human bodies can't be entirely consumed by fire in the open air – Baur himself, who had seen corpses in burning aeroplanes, thought not – and that a proper cremation installation is needed if there are to be no remains. But the place where the bodies were laid was so intensively bombarded by artillery, with flame-throwers and all sorts of weaponry, that it's not surprising if nothing was ever found.

Anyway, the Russians were never in a position to display the remains of Hitler's corpse, as they certainly would have done if they had taken it away, as they claimed. But they did find the body of Goebbels, shrivelled and scarcely recognisable, which they proceeded to put on display: photos of it have been published. I also think that if the Russians had found Hitler's body they wouldn't have gone on interrogating me for so long – not just me, but the others too.

After all this interrogation I was sentenced, together with Linge, Captain Baur and the other officers in Hitler's entourage. I was given twenty-five years in prison (the same sentence was passed on all the Germans in these various trials) although, in fact, apart from the initial period, I spent the whole of my detention in a camp. I was imprisoned for eleven years, almost to the day – until 28 April 1956 – in a 'reform camp', which was a large camp full of prisoners of war. The hardest time was at the beginning, when I was still in prison, in the Lubianka in Moscow, then in Boutirka, both of which are used today as the prisons where the KGB shuts up dissidents. I was there with all sorts of people, mostly German officers, a few Japanese too, and rarely Russians. The regime was very harsh.

In the 'reform camp' there were men of more than twenty different nationalities, including Russian ethnic groups who were being deported to various eastern regions where they were needed as labourers or specialists. But subsequently they were all sentenced and put in camps, where they were used as manual labour. It was there I learnt Russian, first by listening to people and talking to them, then from another German internee, a colonel, who spoke Russian and taught me the rudiments of the language with the aid of a novel by Turgenev. It was hard, since we had neither pencil nor paper nor anything else to write with. I had to try to store it all in my memory. What's more, I was learning nineteenth-century literary Russian, which had very little to do with the Russian that the prisoners around us were speaking. It was as if someone learnt German today from Goethe's *Faust* and then tried to talk to a farm worker who spoke a provincial dialect. I tried to talk to the corporal who came to inspect us every morning, but he didn't even realise I was speaking Russian. He just shook his head, and one of his comrades asked him what language I was using.

When I was set free my first wife, whom I hadn't seen since the war, was dead. But we had a son, who was just a baby when I left them, and I found him again on my return. We were all freed following the first visit to the USSR by Chancellor Adenauer, whose express purpose was to obtain the release of all the prisoners of war the Russians were keeping in the USSR, even some who had never been sentenced.

Otto Günsche is now seventy years old and lives in a small town near Cologne, where he is manager of a pharmaceuticals company.

Hans Baur also endured imprisonment in the Soviet Union. Here is his story:

Although the Führer had told me to leave Berlin immediately, it turned out to be impossible: both the airfields outside Berlin had already fallen to the Russians. Like all the other occupants of the bunkers, I eventually attempted to get out of Berlin on foot. I was badly wounded and had to endure the amputation of one of my legs with a knife.

To add to my troubles, Hitler had awarded me the rank of Lieutenant-General in the Luftwaffe during the last two days in the bunker, and I was unable to convince my Soviet captors that I have never exercised any military function. I was sentenced to twenty-five years in prison in the Soviet Union, and was freed after eleven years, in 1956, when Chancellor Adenauer visited Moscow.

Today Hans Baur lives in a picturesque Bavarian village on the shores of Lake Pilsensee, not far from Munich, where he recently celebrated his ninetieth birthday.

20

Freedom and a New Life

Traudl Junge was released by the Americans in the summer of 1946.

At last I was a totally free woman, and I had to try and remake my life in a new and changed world. Devastating news reports and pictures, as well as the stories of people I met, gradually revealed to me all the horrors of the war – the gas chambers, concentration camps and persecutions that my friendly, fatherly boss and charming, entertaining host at dinner for the last two years had brought about.

The past weighed on my soul much more heavily than the outer deprivations of the period: lack of accommodation, hunger and unemployment. A painful learning process began. In the Russian prisons, where I had expected only hatred and revenge, I was confronted with humanity and assistance and on my return home from prison, the first person to offer me bread and work was a Jewish man named Joachim Hahlweg. He knew that I had been Hitler's secretary but that did not stop him from hiring me. Even when our work together ended – because of external circumstances – I never forgot this gesture of tolerance and conciliation. Through these examples, I came to learn one universal truth: that there are no inferior races or peoples in the world, only good and bad individuals.

Having been brought up in a family where love of the father-land, obedience, sacrifice and the carrying out of duties were considered to be great virtues and having grown up under Hitler's dictatorship, after the war I enjoyed for the first time the happiness of democratic freedom as the newest and most important experience of my life. Being able to think, speak and do what you want without fear, being able to enjoy art, literature and music

165

without considering the race or nationality of the artist: I now consider these to be human rights I would never want to give up again. I could not have guessed how many good things there were which used to be forbidden and which I would now be unable to live without.

Since then I have worked as a secretary and journalist in various editorial offices and publishing companies and I live once more in my home town of Munich – unmarried and childless, but content. Today, whenever I see and hear Hitler in old films and newsreels with those thousands of enthusiastic people cheering him, my heart remains cold. His gestures seem theatrical to me, his words hollow, his poses ridiculous and yet everything I wrote down forty years ago is true. I fell under his spell, gave him my trust and sympathy and felt good when I was near him. We cannot change the past but we can learn from it. I have honestly tried to do so.

I am now nearly seventy years old and everyday I am thankful that I live in peace and freedom in a European community of nations instead of under the supremacy of an arrogant Germanic master race. May there be no more war, no more hate and no more Hitlers!

Index